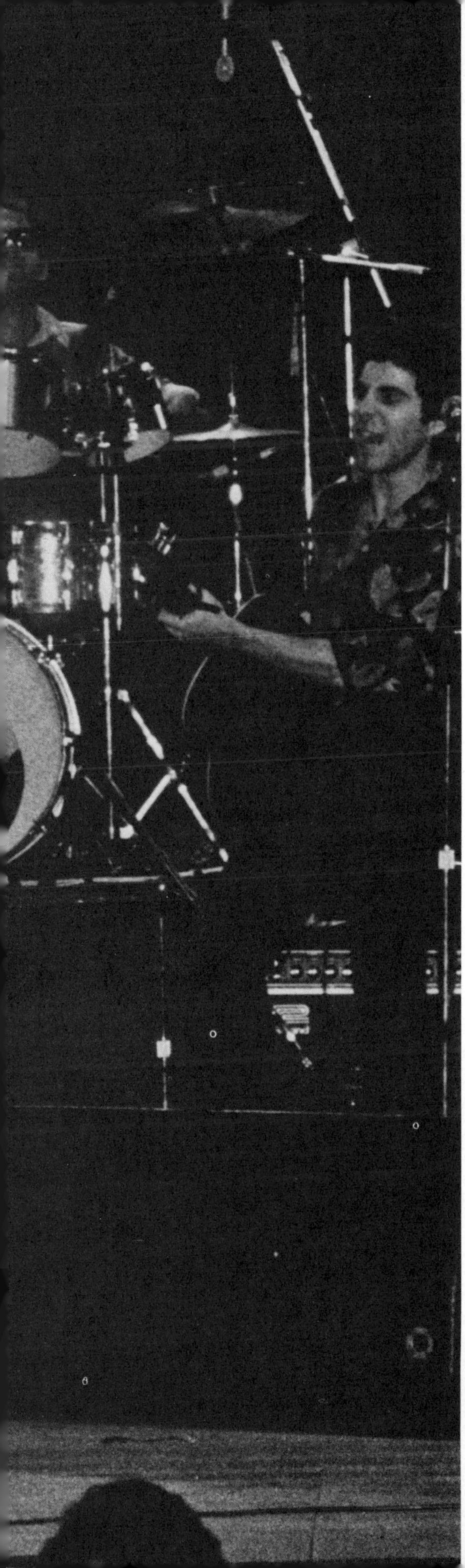

Billy Joel
A PERSONAL FILE

BY PETER GAMBACCINI

Tony Frank/Sygma

NEW YORK • LONDON • TOKYO

CONTENTS

Introduction Page 7
Hicksville Page 11
"Cold Spring Harbor" Page 23
"Streetlife Serenade" Page 39
Back to New York Page 49
"Say Goodbye to Hollywood" Page 61
Elizabeth Page 63
"The Stranger" Page 69
Public Acclaim Page 83
In the Mainstream Page 109
On the Road Page 115
Discography Page 127

Copyright © Quick Fox, 1979
All rights reserved.
Printed in the United States of America.
International Standard Book Number: 0-8256-3940-9
Library of Congress Catalog Card Number: 79-65934

No part of this book may be reproduced or transmitted in any form or by any means, electronic or mechanical, including photocopying, without permission in writing from the publisher: Quick Fox, 33 West 60th Street, New York 10023.

In Great Britain: Book Sales Ltd., 78 Newman Street, London W1P 3LA.

In Canada: Gage Trade Publishing, P.O. Box 5000, 164 Commander Blvd., Agincourt, Ontario M1S 3C7

In Japan: Quick Fox, 4-26-22 Jingumae, Shibuya-ku, Tokyo 150.

Designed by Ede Dreikurs
Cover photographs by David Gahr

Wide World Photos

Tony Frank/Sygma

Jeffrey Mayer

Introduction

In the world of popular music, it may often appear as if enormous wealth and fame are readily at hand for the taking, just waiting to be grabbed up by the newest hot prospect who happens by. Every six months or so, another contender bursts out of nowhere to make a giant impact as the "next big thing." Huge record sales ensue, hordes of media mavens take notice—and more often than not, it is all over in another six months. Lacking substantial talent, experience, and musical foundation, few of these shooting stars have what it takes to maintain such lofty levels in the recording industry for very long.

The music business, however, is not solely comprised of such types. There are also men and women who take a more gradual course to the top. Perhaps they show early promise and then take a little longer than expected to fulfill that promise. Perhaps there are unseen pitfalls, not always of an artistic nature, that slow the artist's progress along the way.

It is a Darwinian universe in which the fittest survive the ones who have enough faith in themselves to keep trying. And the best among them keep trying on *their own terms*. They may be cognizant of trends, booms, and fads, but they don't allow those matters to influence their art. They stick by themselves. If they are both fortunate and gifted, more and more people will take notice at each step along the way.

And then, for the very few, a moment comes, sometimes without inkling or explanation, when what the performer

David Gahr

Chuck Pulin

Chuck Pulin

has to offer and what the public is looking for seem to match perfectly. That performer becomes the "next big thing" —but with a difference. He has toiled in the fields, he has honed his craft, he has more to display than the instant, fleeting brilliance of a comet. There is a vast body of material behind him that the public and other performers are suddenly made aware of. He has, so it is discovered, done a great deal of fine work prior to occupying the spotlight. And he is mature, ready, and creative enough to give a lot more to a populace that now awaits his next move with eager anticipation.

For 1978 and 1979, and for however many years beyond, the long and hard toiler whose time has come is Billy Joel. He has made music all of his adult (and much of his adolescent) life, he has encountered more than a few stumbling blocks along the way, and his reputation has grown noticeably larger until the label of "cult figure" no longer fits. He didn't bow to commercial pressures; he just continued striving to make *his own* music even better. It wasn't punk or disco or New Wave that brought him to the top at the end of the seventies—it was *Billy Joel music*.

The first big breakthrough was "Just The Way You Are," a song that was on so many lovers' lips. "Only The Good Die Young," "My Life," and "Big Shot" were just a part of the chain of huge Joel hits that followed, and his albums *The Stranger* and *52nd Street* became two of the biggest sellers of the decade. By the beginning of 1979, Billy Joel was the premier American solo performer in the whole world of music; add the British to the list and perhaps only Rod Stewart loomed larger than Billy Joel on American song charts.

But as far as the Big Time was concerned, Billy Joel was still the new kid on the block. He gave every indication that his stay in the neighborhood would be a long and fruitful one. He shouldn't surprise anybody if he does even bigger things before he moves out.

CHAPTER I

Hicksville

William Martin Joel was born to Howard and Rosalind Joel in the Bronx on May 9, 1949, but grew up in Hicksville, Long Island. The family resided in the West Village section of Hicksville's Levittown. Joel, of German-English heritage, grew up in a neighborhood that was largely Irish, Polish, and Italian.

Hicksville and Levittown and the other communities that form the heart of Nassau County on Long Island are every bit as aesthetically desolate as their reputation suggests. The Levittown area where Billy grew up was the kind of planned community that was to become infamous and synonymous with soulless suburbs—block after block of houses without character, virtually identical to each other. It's not surprising that the product of such an environment would later write "Captain Jack," one of the most merciless condemnations of suburban adolescense ever recorded.

The housing pattern that has come to be epitomized by the mere word "Levittown"—the small indistinguishable homes on tiny lots in long rows—is by no means confined to Levittown itself. It dominates many of the Long Island towns that prospered after the Second World War. To live there could hardly provide all the positive stimuli a creative individual requires.

"There's an identity crisis," Billy would tell writer Dave Marsh. "You're a nothing, you're a zero in the suburbs. You're mundane, you're common. You have 2.4 children, you have a quarter-acre plot of land, you have a Ford Wagoneer. Who gives a damn about you?"

"The first thing on your mind when you got older," Joel told *Newsweek*'s Maureen Orth, "was to escape—to get out of doing the same thing and seeing the same houses everywhere you look."

German-born Howard Joel was a General Electric engineer with a love of classical music. When Billy's parents

Richard E. Aaron

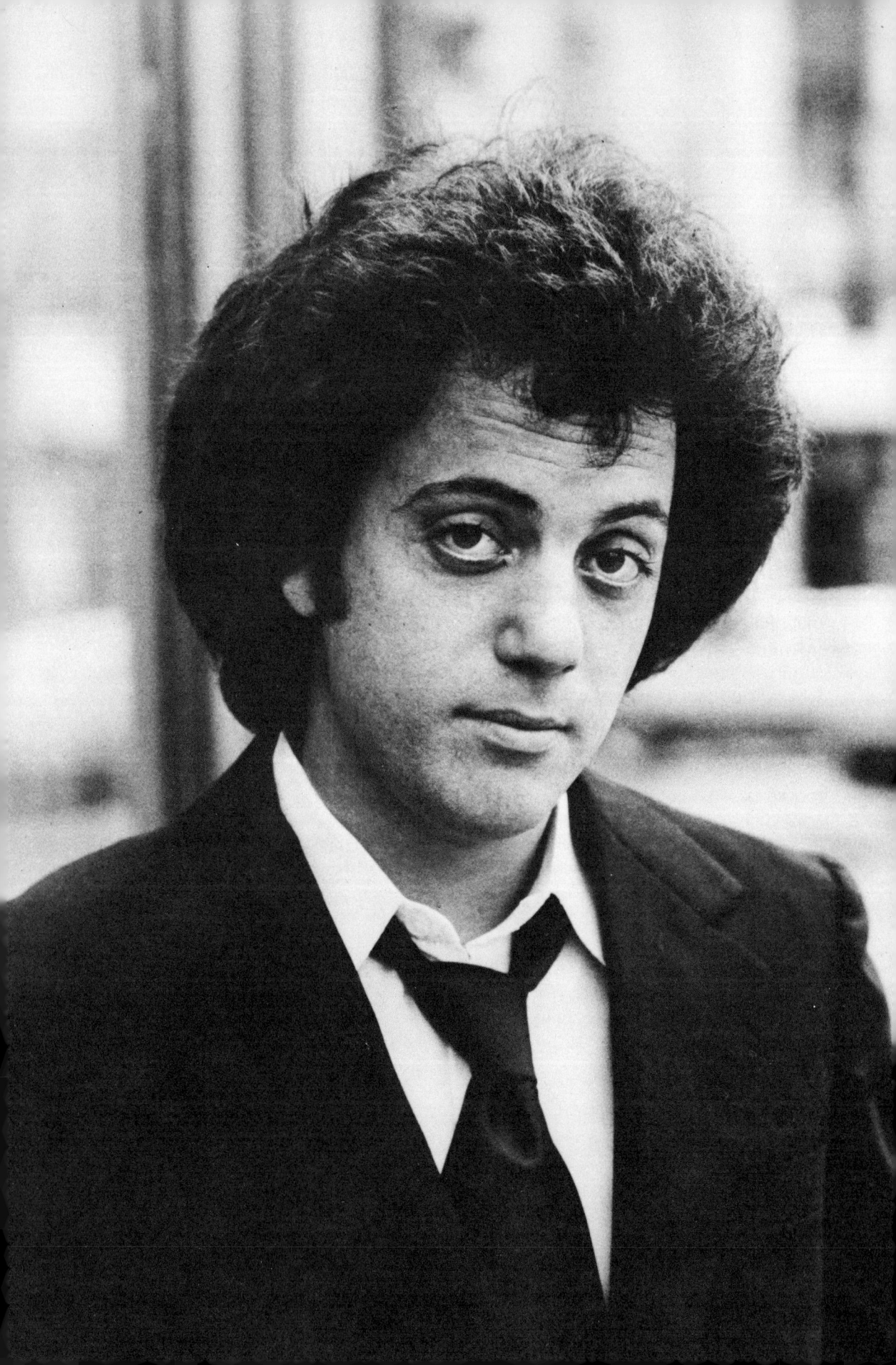

noted that their four-year-old son was showing a keen interest in a Mozart selection, they signed the boy up for piano lessons. His improvisational proclivities were not encouraged, however. Once, playing a Beethoven sonata, he "started boogie-woogieing to it. And my old man came downstairs and smacked the hell outta me."

Billy's father left home and returned to Europe when his son was only seven years old. It remained for mother Rosalind to raise Billy and his sister Judy on her secretary's salary. Meanwhile, Billy continued his classical lessons for about a dozen years.

"As I got older I realized that if you're going to be a concert pianist, then you've got to practice six hours a day and devote your whole life to it," he told *High Fidelity* writer-editor Susan Elliot. "You become a high-strung maniac.... It just seems to be so competitive. It doesn't seem to be a lot of fun. And I wanted to have fun."

He added in a *Rolling Stone* conversation with Dave Marsh, "I never wanted to be Vladimir Horowitz. I never really enjoyed playing the classics, although I'm glad I did."

As a youngster, Billy planned to be a history teacher. For much of his boyhood there was no TV in the house, so he read a slew of history books, along with novels. "A lot of my romanticism comes from novelists," he has said, citing F. Scott Fitzgerald, Ernest Hemingway, Mark Twain, Jean-Paul Sartre, Franz Kafka, and Hermann Hesse.

As a junior-high-school hood, Billy said in *Feature*, he would "run over the green to sniff glue, drink Tango wine, and screw around with the gang. We'd all seen *West Side Story* and wore purple shirts like Bernardo did."

It wasn't all innocent fun. "We'd hit places, rob stores at night. A lot of friends of mine went to jail, and some got killed by getting hit by trains, or by getting really bombed on glue, walking on a trestle and falling off onto the parkway. Really crazed-out stuff."

In *People* he noted that he was once picked up on suspicion of burglary, "which pissed me off because they didn't get me all the other times."

At times, however, Joel conveys the impression that his activities were not all that out of the ordinary. "I wasn't like Al Capone like some of these screwies make out to be, fighting all my life," Billy declared in a *Newsday* interview. "I was an average kid, and I did what every other kid did."

The choices for a Long Island lad in those days weren't numerous, as Billy indicated in *Time*. "You got into junior high, you could go one of three ways. You could be a collegiate, a hitter, or a brownie—the kid who wears brown shoes with white socks, carries a schoolbag, and always gets the monitor jobs."

Like everyone his age, Billy was listening to a lot of music, but his tastes were discriminating. "A lot of the records I thought were stupid," he informed Susan Elliot. "I liked Phil Spector records, the old Sam & Dave stuff, James Brown, Otis Redding."

Billy joined his first rock outfit, the Echoes, in 1964. "We were hitters, I mean I had a gang and that's what we did" he recalls of the period. "They called us punks—we didn't call ourselves punks—we thought we were hoods. I was called a punk when I started because a real wise guy is a punk. I remember they called Elvis Presley a punk—and I thought the Young Rascals were punks!"

"I was at that age when you try to get 'dis girl to come outside with you," Billy told Timothy White in *Feature*. "And if you're horny enough you'll tell somebody anything: 'Please! Forget all that stuff your mother and the nuns told you! I am right and they are wrong. *I've got to get into your pants!*' " Recollections of those urges and frustrations would later be the partial basis for "Only The Good Die Young," a bit hit for Joel.

With his father gone and his mother working at a variety of jobs, Billy needed the income the music provided. As a teen-ager he frequently gigged at clubs late into the evening, dragging himself to his high school classes in a state of exhaustion. Billy was red-eyed from his late performances and his hair was sufficiently long for folks to believe he was "a drug addict," he explained to *People* magazine's Jim Jerome. "It was just that I worked hard."

The band life led to frequent absence from high school classes, and for that reason he did not graduate with his classmates in 1967.

"I knew from the time I was 14, when I started being a professional musician, making money as a musician, that I was not going to live an ordinary kinda life," he said to Dave Marsh. "I knew I could make a living as a musician. Money, I never had a desire for."

The Echoes were to become the Lost Souls and then the Emerald Lords. Superstardom didn't exactly overwhelm them, and Billy and his bass player moved, in 1968, to a group called the Hassles. The Hassles did two records for United Artists, "The Hassles" and "Hour of the Wolf." Billy's term for the latter one is "psychedelic bullshit."

The mid-sixties were a golden period for suburban New York rock bands. Few enjoyed national renown, but a number of them were winning legions of local worshippers and were playing surprisingly sophisticated rock at an early age.

The Young Rascals, later to be called merely the Rascals, were the most successful at extending their reputation beyond the New York area. Led by Felix Cavaliere, this quartet of three Italians and a WASP, who initially appeared in public

Dr. John, Billy Joel, and Eliot Murphy at the Bottom Line, 1977.

wearing Buster Brownish "mean-wittle-kid" outfits as befits their moniker, were probably the biggest Top-40 rock band in the nation at their zenith, with hits like "Groovin'," "I Ain't Gonna Eat Out My Heart Anymore," "Good Lovin'," and "A Girl Like You." Oddly enough in the late seventies, as Billy Joel is becoming one of the biggest musical names in the land, much of the Rascals' material is finding its way back into the repertoire of new young East Coast bands.

Other groups making the rounds in Long Island, Westchester, and Connecticut at the time included Vanilla Fudge, with Tim Bogart, Mark Stein, and Carmen Appice, who made an impact nationally with "You Keep Me Hanging On." That song, originally a Supremes hit, was done again in 1977 by Rod Stewart, who (these things get involved) by that time had added Carmen Appice to his band. The Rich Kids and the Vagrants were the other leading local lights; the Vagrants featured a porcine guitarist named Leslie Weinstein, who as Leslie West was to later amass a fortune as the frontman of Mountain.

By 1970, Billy was leaving with Hassles' drummer Jon Small to make a duo; duos were big in those days. This one, however, had the somewhat inhospitable name of Attila. They did convince Epic to release one of their albums in July of that year. The titles were terrific; "Brain Invasion," "Revenge Is Sweet," and "Amplifier Fire" were a few examples. You probably never heard the album, but if you are among those rare folks who own a copy you might consider a public auction. Many record dealers who know Billy Joel is a hot ticket and who are accustomed to selling rare items for five times their list price aren't even aware of this album. The cover of the only Attila album shows Billy and drummer Small dressed in Hun outfits, surrounded by slabs of red beef.

With Attila, Billy was primarily playing the organ, and his vocals in this raucous duo nearly amounted to yelling. Finally he decided, "I can't sing like this all the time. This is crazy!" His desire was to quit performing and just compose songs, but things rarely work that way in modern show business.

When Attila failed to make him a household word, he added to his music income by an assortment of jobs. He painted Locust Valley's Piping Rock Country Club, had a stint in a factory, did some criticism for *Changes* magazine, and even recorded a commercial for Bachmann pretzels with Chubby Checker.

"At one point when I was about 21, I lost my girl, the music thing wasn't happening, everything was going wrong," he related to White. "I went through this self-pity stage, really feeling sorry for myself. Life was lousy, adulthood was creeping up on me, I was thinking I was going to be suicidal. And so I checked myself into a nuthouse."

The place in question was Meadowbrook Hospital in East Meadow, Long Island, a place Joel claims was "just like *One Flew Over the Cuckoo's Next*. They take off all your clothes and give you this smock to wear—with your ass sticking out. You can't have any cigarette lighters or razor blades."

The place was rife with people trying to get off alcohol or drugs, with all sorts of deluded creatures; "one guy thinks he's Napoleon and another could be a homocidal maniac."

The routine was not exhilarating. "You get up in the morning and they give you Thorazine. You have breakfast, and they give you another tranquilizer. You have lunch, then you watch a little TV; have dinner, they give you another pill, and you go to sleep."

"At the end of three weeks, I had to sit and talk to these shrinks and convince them I shouldn't be there," Joel recalled in a *Feature* article. "I said, 'Look, hey, I'm OK. I really am.'

"They showed me inkblots, and I said, 'They look like inkblots to me. Believe me! *Let me out of here!*'"

Joel observed, "I guess that's what they wanted to hear. And once I got out of there, I thought it was like, 'OK, Jack, no matter what happens, 'dose people are crazy and you're not. You may be crazy, but not like that.'"

Joel's reflection on that time is that "there's just a time when you feel so isolated and sorry for yourself, and almost nobody can help you. Even if you have somebody else, there comes a time when you feel totally alone. That's the worst thing you can do—feel so sorry for yourself that you can't think straight anymore."

The next phase of the scuffling Joel's career came after he signed with an organization called Family Productions in 1971. Through the joint efforts of that outfit and Just Sunshine, Inc., Billy recorded his first solo album of his own compositions. The record *Cold Spring Harbor* is generally listed as a Paramount album, but it was actually distributed by Famous Music Corporation, which, like Paramount, is a Gulf + Western Company.

Cold Spring Harbor, named for a village on Long Island's north shore, was produced by Artie Ripp and has Billy playing piano, organ, harpsichord, and harmonica. Recorded at Record Plant West and at Ultrasonic Recording Studios, and with arrangements by Jimmie Haskell, *Cold Spring Harbor* showcases Billy surrounded by some very high-priced studio musicians. They include some of the most sought-after talents of the era, including legendary steel guitarist Sneaky Pete Kleinow (of the Flying Burrito Brothers, among others), drummer Denny Siewell, and bassists Joe Osborn (whose credits must number in the thousands) and Larry Knechtel, a versatile stalwart who was part of the successful group Bread. The rest of the cast includes Rhys Clark on drums and Don Evans and Sal DeTrois on guitars.

The album art is all black and white. Hero Billy leans against a pier somewhere on the Long Island shore, looking sloe-eyed and somber. With a blown-dry hairstyle and a very thick dark mustache, he bears a remarkable resemblance to the late Freddie Prinze.

Cold Spring Harbor made minimal sales impact when it first appeared, and it virtually disappeared from circulation by the time Billy Joel emerged as a star of the highest magnitude at the end of 1977. When that level of fame was achieved, however, the once obscure *Cold Spring Harbor* began to reappear in selected stores. As an out-of-print album by a minor performer who had now become extremely major, *Cold Spring Harbor* was easily commanding prices in the neighborhood of $20.

Cold Spring Harbor is of value chiefly because it presents the performing and composing genius of Billy Joel in its fledgling stages. The quality here, in every area, is nowhere near that of his first Columbia album, which would come just two years later. But there are intermittent flashes of brilliance, musical foreshadowings of things to come, and hints of the influences that were to shape the man's grander accomplishments.

Generally, the performances are thinner and the production tinnier than one would hope for. The first track, "She's Got A Way," suffers from both flaws. This is a devotional to an unnamed woman; the instrumental backing is quite minimal, as Billy's rather simple and basic piano playing is virtually unadorned.

The very young Billy, who was probably just twenty-two when this session was recorded, sounds more like a boy

soprano here than on any other selection released under his name. His voice had obviously not yet reached full maturity. "She's Got A Way" is very unexceptional. It's a typical romantic tune, with rhymes that are extremely obvious from beginning to end.

"You Can Make Me Free," at 5:40 the only song on the first side over four minutes long, is a bit of an improvement. It is a tribute to his lover's power over him, her seemingly superhuman ability to control great destinies, his in particular.

It would be easy to call this track Beatlesque, but as with most of the Liverpudlians' emulators, Joel sounds more like the other copyists than like the real item. "You Can Make Me Free" could be a lost track from an Emmitt Rhodes album, or anything by Eric Carmen and the Raspberries.

There are some interesting keyboard effects here and a good guitar that unfortunately gets out of control. In fact, the long instrumental denouement, combined with Beatlesque vocal harmonies, is poorly balanced and very cacophonous. Over all this, is some lyric shouting by Billy that is much in the style of Paul McCartney.

The fast-paced "Everybody Loves You Now" is quite a bit better and might even be worth resurrecting in the current Joel repertoire. It is far less of a paean than the first two tunes; it is the first example we'd yet heard of the very telling Joel sardonicism.

The fast, rumbling piano and acoustic guitar intro is similar to much of the material on the *Piano Man* album, and the lyric is smug and accusatory. The person being addressed appears to be in a position of celebrity, an idol of worship to unnamed throngs. With a fine dramatic vocal delivery, a slightly bitter Billy warns of impending loneliness, fleeting fame, and undesirable personality changes that will ensue. Beyond all that, it is obvious that this is someone, almost certainly a woman, from whom he is now sadly estranged. There are personal references to the Staten Island Ferry and to Cold Spring Harbor that indicate past intimacies in a way that recognizes that they are *past*.

The song is executed at such a high speed that it seems a tirade of sorts; there's no miserable wallowing here. Clearly he knows he must pick up and go on. The attitude is mature, and likewise there is an inkling of a maturing talent at work here.

"Why Judy Why" is very romantic and tender, soft, and has a Spanish feel. "Of all the people in the world that I know / You're the best place to go," he exclaims unabashedly. This is a faltering relationship, and Billy only begins to acknowledge his need for Judy when she becomes less accessible. The effect on him seems devastating: "A man my age is very young, so I'm told / Why do I feel so old?" There is a nicely done guitar duet, exotic and mournful and apt. Some of the language in this song could have been polished up, but the notion of a man emotionally falling to pieces is effectively conveyed. "There's no tomorrow 'cause my dream did not last," moans poor Billy.

On "Falling Of The Rain," which wraps up side one, Billy's cascading piano opening, masterfully brisk, leads to a fairy tale of the "once upon a time" variety. In a voice that could be a little stronger, we hear of a painter who does nice work but can't hear the falling of the rain, and of a braided, lovely girl who hears it and doesn't mind a bit.

This gets to be a very lyrically ambitious parable; the two characters come to stand for Billy and a girl he's pursuing. His efforts appear unsuccessful, and she goes away. "The falling of the rain" would seem to represent the natural passage of time, real life in essence. He can't seem to acknowledge it, and that's where he's beaten.

No one has talked much about Billy Joel as a symbolist, and maybe there is no reason to take such a discussion very far. There is symbolism in "Falling Of The Rain," however. The fantastic imagery of the first verses is far more gripping than the real-life situation he later introduces. A potentially interesting tale becomes one about which we are likely to remark "Oh, is that all?"

Sneaky Pete's pedal steel is featured on "Turn Around," which is western-tinged, like several *Piano Man* tracks. There is a recurring metaphor of a woman as a running river, but the lyrics are not very intriguing. The piano parts are very derivative of many popular records of the day, particularly the work of Pete Sears and Ian McLagan on the first two Rod Stewart solo albums. Enough said; "Turn Around" is not very original or impressive.

With a very jaunty organ opening, "You Look So Good To Me" is reminiscent of the "good-time" music purveyed by such mellow freaks as The Lovin' Spoonful and The Cyrcle a few years earlier. By a long shot, this is the most optimistic song on *Cold Spring Harbor.* The woman Billy is singing to can do no wrong. She's full of pleasant surprises, and she makes him feel happy, warm, free, and whatever else he desires. What's more, the two of them seem to be getting along famously. Nothing to complain about here.

"You Look So Good To Me" may be a tad trivial, but it is archetypal pop music that, with slightly clearer production and more promotion, might have been a hit single five years earlier. Among other things, it shows that Billy Joel is an astute observer of American popular music history.

The bravura performance of side two, and the longest cut at 4:47, is "Tomorrow Is Today." Like "She's Got A Way," it opens with very spartan piano fingering. A man who has lived for the moment begins to sense that the moments have passed too quickly. The days become indistinguishable: "I don't have to see tomorrow 'cause I saw it yesterday." Dreams seem useless; the next morning promises nothing, and his woman won't take the love he's giving. There's nothing new in this life. Billy ought to go out and make some new friends.

After this dreary scene unfolds, Joel suddenly breaks into a far more soulful, deeper voice for a scant few bars. This supplies a bit of drama where it's needed in this long and dolorous song. It is also early evidence of the versatility of the Joel vocal cords; he could be any of a number of macho crooners.

This brief outburst serves as a kind of catharsis, and Billy is soon back to sighing and moaning, which he continues to do until the song comes to an end. "Tomorrow Is Today" rates a "not bad," maybe six on a scale of one to ten. You would encourage this fellow to keep at it.

The piano solo "Nocturne" (with minor orchestral support) is a reminder from Billy that he in fact was paying attention during those twelve years of classical lessons. His chords are full and rich. This is an original composition, but very much in the Chopin vein. There is one section near the end where he heads into a more popular mode, but he brings it back to high art. "Nocturne" is a very appropriate 2:37 instrumental interlude. It would be welcome on any Billy Joel album, or as a cooling break after a particularly hot concert selection.

As he was to do frequently in his career with Columbia, Billy ends his album on a quiet note with a song that suggests a need for temporary solitude, a sense of direction, and general rebirth. The soft "Got To Begin Again" is eerily prophetic. A fledgling talent has come to

Michael Putland/Retna

the end of his first album, a good experience and a nice introduction to the business, but one that was not about to make him a household word. And here he is saying,

*"Here I am at the end of the road.
Where do I go from here?
I always figured it would be like this
But nothing seems to be quite clear."*

What to do for an encore, that is the question. The rest of the lyrics have a larger application—again some struggling romance figures in—for they are very apt when one thinks of what good times and bad awaited young Mr. Joel. The title is "Got To Begin Again," and that is exactly what he would have to do, several times in fact, before he was to become the most publicly acclaimed piano man of the late seventies.

There is some strong stuff on *Cold Spring Harbor*. "Everybody Loves You Now" and "Nocturne" are unquestionable successes, and "Why Judy Why," "Falling Of The Rain," and "Got To Begin Again," among others, showed that here was a knowledgeable young musicmaker who was on the right track and might be expected to "get it right" in the near future. The singing and the playing were promising, needed improvement, and would undoubtedly *get* what they needed. And, as is even truer of Peter Townshend of The Who, Billy Joel showed us melodic strains that would be echoed in compositions yet to come. With time to mature, a bigger budget, and the support of a major record company, this Joel fellow would probably do all right for himself.

Cold Spring Harbor would be a decent enough buy at list price; for the Joel fanatic or the serious student of popular music, it is worth having, to see that even on vinyl mighty oaks grow from tiny acorns. Now if you can just find *Cold Spring Harbor* for less than $20, you'll be all set.

Be advised, however, that one fairly major thing did go amiss in the making of *Cold Spring Harbor*. Billy explained to *Penthouse* writer William Kowinski, "Once the album was finished, it got speeded up in the mastering process—the machine was going ten cycles faster than it was supposed to. So by the time they finished pressing 50,000 copies, my voice sounded like a chipmunk. They sent me a copy. I was living on Long Island in Oyster Bay. I put the record on. My friends were there, cracking up laughing."

Michael Putland/Retna

CHAPTER 2

"Cold Spring Harbor"

Chuck Pulin

Rock stardom wasn't Billy's goal with *Cold Spring Harbor*; he wanted to be known as a songwriter. "All the advice I got from people in the music business was: 'You want people to hear your songs, why don't you make a record. This way, people will hear your songs,'" he said, in a *Rolling Stone* piece by Dave Marsh.

Billy was persuaded to go on the road to promote the album; he did so for six months, but unfortunately, he was not given the best of backup bands for his tour, and Paramount's efforts to promote *Cold Spring Harbor* didn't do the job. Quickly Billy split for the West Coast, settling rather anonymously, in North Hollywood with girlfriend (and later wife) Elizabeth.

He toured a bit with a band, but that endeavor was less than prosperous. For six months, under the name Bill Martin, he played in the piano bar of a Los Angeles cocktail lounge called the Executive Room. As Martin he seemed to be an entirely different persona; for five hours each evening, he would play this role in what he admitted to Marsh was an alcohol-induced daze.

Bill Martin was "a good draw," according to Angelique Norton, who with her husband Russell owned the Executive Room while Joel entertained there. In *Feature*, she recalled, "He had a following. On slow nights I'd ask him to play some of the classics, like a polonaise by

23

Chopin, and he'd do them. But he used to tell me he didn't like having to play requests for people. Sometimes customers would start singing along and he definitely didn't like that, either."

After a time, Joel left North Hollywood for a remote mountain home near Malibu. There he set about the serious business of writing new songs.

However, a tape of "Captain Jack," a song written while Joel still lived in Long Island, surfaced and got airplay back east.

Philadelphia's most important progressive radio station, WMMR-FM, played a vital role in the career of Billy Joel, as it has done for several deserving musicians. In the days when he was being generally ignored by most programmers, WMMR-FM had played a lot of Bruce Springsteen music, making The Boss a popular fave in the Philadelphia area even before he was big in New York.

The station did much the same for Joel, thanks to a 1972 live broadcast of a concert which featured a crowd-pleasing performance of "Captain Jack." A tape of that song was aired on the station to popular demand for several months, even though Joel had yet to put it on an album.

"Captain Jack" earned the status of an underground hit, and for some time Joel was intermittently referred to as "Philadelphia Billy Joel" by many folks, even though he is in no way a Pennsylvanian.

What mattered most, of course, was what the record company folks thought. Executives from Columbia had seen and been impressed by Billy at Puerto Rico's Mar y Sol Rock Festival, and they were familiar with the Philadelphia concert broadcast and the reception given "Captain Jack." The company pursued Billy to California and signed him to a contract in the spring of 1973.

Later Billy would say he never even saw copies of *Cold Spring Harbor* in the stores. And of his business arrangement with Family Productions, he has said "I signed a lot of stupid papers . . . I signed away my publishing and my copyrights." In California, his answer to them was to "just sit them out. If they finally realized that they weren't going to get anything out of me, maybe they'd negotiate a new contract."

Joel was able to get a better arrangement with them when Columbia chief Clive Davis started to express interest in him. Although Davis set in motion the deal with Joel, he left before it was final and Kip Cohen actually signed Billy to the label.

The Columbia debut, *Piano Man,* was recorded at Devonshire Sound in North Hollywood, with Michael Stewart producing, Ron Malo engineering, and Michael Omartian and Jimmie Haskell supplying the arrangements. Joel played all the keyboards, and he was surrounded by many of the finest available West Coast musicians.

The only holdover from the *Cold Spring Harbor* sessions was drummer Rhys Clark. Eric Weissberg, who had the novelty hit "Dueling Banjos" from *Deliverance,* played some banjo here. Two members of the Crusaders, the acclaimed all-star jazz outfit, were on hand —guitarist Larry Carlton and bassist Wilton Felder.

Omartian himself played occasional accordion. The rest of the line-up featured guitarists Richard Bennett and Dean Parks, bassist Emory Gordy, drummer Ron Tutt, banjo player Fred Heilbrun, fiddler Billy Armstrong, and background vocalists billed as The Creamers/ Susan Steward & Co.

Piano Man was released on November 9, 1973. The single of the same name had come out a week earlier; largely on the strength of that, the record stayed on the charts through the first part of 1974 and eventually won certification as a gold album.

The brown-toned cover of *Piano Man*

has Billy Joel appearing in what seems to be a death mask; the illustration, by Bill Imhoff, shows a facial oval of stark features and pallid skin peering out from the darkness. On the back, the ghostly apparition of Billy is gray, although his eyes are still brown, and scraggly hair seems to have been penciled in.

With staccato precision of drums, then bass, and finally piano, "Travellin' Prayer" opens the first side of *Piano Man*. This is the most secular of prayers and a spectacularly lively number. This is a textured performance that piles layer on instrumental layer from start to finish, and the proceedings never get out of hand.

There is a liberal dose of Wild Western motif on this album, and "Travellin' Prayer" contains enough banjo, fiddle, and occasional honky-tonk piano to make it seem that the journeying here is by stagecoach.

Joel, the disciple, is requesting the Lord's protection for his love "far across the sea." Make her dreams sweet, make the roads soft for her feet, but mainly, bring her home to Billy.

Billy and his lively backup band seem to act as sentinels, properly supplying this unnamed lass with all the protection she could need. As one danger after another is mentioned in the lyric, one instrumentalist after another comes forward, brandishing the weapon he handles best.

Billy rattles off all the pitfalls that may engulf the sojourner along the way, and his anxiety increases, partly because he's begging for help from a Supreme Being with whom he rarely communicates.

A short solo at midpoint shows how far Billy's piano technique had come since *Cold Spring Harbor*, and a sizzling bit of fiddling by Billy Armstrong answers him in fine style.

"Travellin' Prayer" masterfully conveys a lover's sense of urgency and impatience for a geographical separation to end. The trepidation is always greater for the person who is waiting than for the one who is on the move, and that is very much the case here.

The lyric demands our attention, but in the meantime, Billy and the boys are truly playing up a storm. When the song reaches its logical conclusion, they're still hot, so after a pause of a moment or two, a second instrumental finale comes on.

"Travellin' Prayer" is fast-paced, well-executed, and a great opener for Joel's first Columbia album.

Now that we know him a little, we get to know him a lot in the title tune "Piano Man," which would be his signature song for years, easily his best known number until he was to become a phenomenally popular performer nearly five years later.

"Piano Man" draws much of its inspiration from Billy's days as a Los Angeles lounge entertainer, although the accordion strains provided by Michael Omartian occasionally suggest the flavor of a Paris bistro. The cast of characters drawn in "Piano Man" includes many representative types whose real-life counterparts probably spent a lot of time slumped over Joel's keyboard in the L.A. bar. The piano man's locale seems to be a less than cheery one, and the pianist plays the role of psychiatrist to a larger extent than the proverbial bartender.

There is a very large cast and plenty of human emotion packed into 5:37 here. Oddly enough, the one-handed piano tinkering of the intro suggests the laziness of a late hour, but as Billy soon informs us "it's nine o'clock on a Saturday."

Billy's eyes perceive the patrons, first encountering an old man "making love to his tonic and gin," who wants a song he knew "when I wore a younger man's clothes." There's John, the witty bartender, who has "someplace that he'd rather be"; like everyone else in the room, he is in a trap of his own making. A similar fate engulfs the "real estate novelist" and the Navy lifer.

It is to Billy they look for solace ("you've got us feelin' all right") and perhaps for inspiration. But the piano man, we begin to learn, has his own frustrations, something that Joel's lyrics only begin to tell after the song is halfway done. Although the patrons who admire his talents ask, "man what are you doing here?", it is clearly a question he has asked himself many a time. A lot of his own pain is in this song.

"Piano Man" is picturesque; we can see Billy sitting there, playing a lot better than is ever warranted in a piano lounge, taking in everything he sees and thinking, "someday I'll write about this." His fingers may be working at the bar, but his heart and his dreams are elsewhere.

In "Piano Man" everyone is a failure, or at least unfulfilled. While Joel isn't overly critical of their state, neither is he sympathetic, at least not on the basis of this evidence.

"Piano Man" was so clearly autobiographical that it didn't take long for folks to associate the real-life Billy with the narrator of this song. It is an impression that has stuck. That has advantages and disadvantages; it is nice to be recognized on the basis of such a song, but people might not have realized that Billy's repertoire was far more vast and varied than this one song indicated.

On the positive side, "Piano Man" shows early on that Joel has great strength as a teller of tales, that he vividly brings characters and situations to life. Microcosmic as the world of the "Piano Man" might be, the anguish and dissatisfaction in that piano bar are universal. In this song, Billy creates a kind of stationary *Ship of Fools*.

After two very impressive tracks, "Ain't No Crime" is the weak link on this album's first side. Basically it lets us know that sometimes it's okay to stay out late and get smashed even if your woman doesn't like it; such is human nature. Your penance, of course, is that in the morning, nine o'clock comes "without any warning."

There is one good bit of wisdom here; as Billy observes of relationships, "you may love her forever, but you won't like her every day." Especially on the days when she kvetches about the hours you keep.

With a female backing chorus and Billy's roaring vocal, there is a suggestion of soulfulness on "Ain't No Crime." But the music, despite a thundering bass and a reasonably good but uncredited sax solo, is rambunctious without being riveting, and the result is a garbled mishmash. "Ain't No Crime" is one of *Piano Man*'s lesser selections.

"You're My Home" is not one of the best known Billy Joel songs; it is somewhere in the middle as far as fame goes. It gets played fairly often but not so much that you memorize every nuance of it. But it is the kind of song that can be covered especially by lesser Las Vegas-style entertainers. It also is the song which started Joel's reputation as a romantic, even though that is only one portion of his nature.

"You're My Home" begins with a trickling guitar part much like the opening of "Everybody's Talking" from *Midnight Cowboy*." The basis of the song is an endearing if old romantic cliché. Billy, the boy with wanderlust and perhaps even no fixed address, has at least one place he can call home, and that place is his woman.

Electronic keyboards and twangy guitars give the effect of a rolling river, one that wanders and meanders just like Billy. The tune and the words are perfect

Tin Pan Alley fare from an earlier age. Joel tells of the "crazy gypsy in my soul" and notes,

*"I never had a place that I could call my own
but that's alright my love 'cause you're my home."*

Whether it be Pennsylvania, Indiana, or California, "home is just another word for you."

With its very simple instrumentation and hardly new premise, "You're My Home" might just be sappy stuff if it weren't for some clever literary references ("you're my instant pleasure dome") and clear indications that these are flesh-and-blood humans that do a lot more than just pine for each other and get misty-eyed. The weary Billy has a friend who understands his needs:

*"Use my body for your bed
and my love will keep you warm throughout the night."*

This is an adult love story about real people; there's no ludicrous "oh come now" idealism. It's not an ivory tower relationship; it's street-people stuff.

The closing piece on side one, "The Ballad of Billy The Kid," is absolutely terrific. Jimmie Haskell's arrangement combines the Western idiom with orchestral spectacle and import.

"Billy The Kid" is perfect from beginning to end. The opening cello chords give the feeling of a day dawning on the plains, and the hoof-clomping percussion and cowboy harmonica rhythms that follow give us fair warning that a formidable sodbuster has come to town. The calm is broken by some very jarring guitar and well-coordinated, four-limbed drumming. Joel heralds the arrival of the man from "the town known as Wheeling, West Virginia."

This song would have to be called cowboy rock because it's about cowboys and it truly rocks, but it forges a territory all its own. In a superb lyric worthy of any old Ned Buntline dime-novel myth, Joel tells the step-by-step saga of the young and small fellow whose "daring life of crime made him a legend in his time."

The whole story is there, of this fellow whom many will speak of but few will know, as he robs and shoots "from Utah to Oklahoma." It's all told against an instrumental background that is appropriately bombastic, with searing guitar, bellowing French horn, magnificent strings, and a nimble variety of piano tricks by Billy Joel, who musically carries on a dialogue with each of the other instruments. He holds his own and never misses a beat. The man can play anything he's called on to play.

Joel the storyteller has a good sense of detail, making us appreciate Billy the Kid as a loner and a man who was capable of generating some weird form of respect. His inevitable downfall assumes some dimension of tragedy, and the hopeless misfit finally finds a home "underneath the Boot Hill grave that bears his name."

Billy Joel, who was only twenty-four when he recorded "The Ballad of Billy The Kid," was obviously already an accomplished student of songwriting and of variegated musical forms. "Billy The Kid" is a complex piece, almost symphonic. There are an enormous number of elements here, little bits that have to fit together to make it work, and it *does* work.

Joel has a deft sense of timing and drama. And his fascination with the late William Bonney (Billy the Kid) becomes explicable. Before the last notes of The Kid's saga can be heard, almost as soon as he is nestling into that Boot Hill grave, this becomes the ballad of Billy Joel, "from the town known as Oyster Bay, Long Island." Presumably, Oyster Bay is more the stuff of legend than Hicksville or Levittown. Here, riding with "a six pack in his hand," is another cocky kid, undoubtedly, in his own milieu, capable of putting "older guns to shame."

The Bonney-Joel analogy comes suddenly and without warning but seems not at all out of place; it is very striking. Like the man he's eulogizing, Billy Joel wants to be a legend "east and west of the Rio Grande."

"The Ballad of Billy The Kid" is a stunner; who could ask for anything more? Its sound is completely fresh, not a retread or derivative of too familiar material. Joel's saga is strong, evocative, and gripping.

What would have happened if he'd played Alias, Bob Dylan's role, and written the soundtrack for Sam Peckinpah's *Pat Garrett and Billy The Kid*? It's worth wondering about; Joel certainly would have been another gun to contend with, and he'd probably be fulfilling a few fantasies in the process.

"Worse Comes To Worse" begins side two and captures Billy in a mood of engaging nonchalance. The guitar opening, probably by Carlton, has the kind of chug-a-chug licks very familiar in current "fusion" music, but when "Worse Comes To Worse" gets under way it is a light and bouncy Latin number; you can even hear a marimba in the background.

*"Today I'm living like a rich man's son
Tomorrow morning I could be a bum,"*

notes Billy, keenly aware that the promise and riches of a Columbia recording star could very well be fleeting.

So what does he think about it? Well, he's not upset; if he doesn't have a car he'll hitch, and he can always make a living in a piano bar. Nothing will get this boy down, because although the possible pitfalls he lists are quite real, he offers up his panacea repeatedly; "I know a woman in New Mexico." If the worst happens, that's where he'll go.

"Worse Comes To Worse" includes one line of cogent Joel philosophy that is also a piece of personal prophecy.

*"Fun ain't easy if it ain't free
Too many people got a hold on me,"*

sings Billy, enjoying the notion of being a musician on a major record label, but very much aware of his entangled business affairs.

Nevertheless, this track comes off as a piece of unbridled optimism; it's one of those days when nothing can get him down. Along with the various Ray Davies' "it's a sunny day, what could possibly be the matter" ditties, this is a good song to put on when gloom and doom seem to be setting in. And Joel the pianist handles the south-of-the-border riffs very nicely, as he continues to demonstrate on *Piano Man* that he is a master of many styles.

Up next is "Stop in Nevada," a well-orchestrated, country-tinged tune about an unhappy wife who finally gets up and splits. Like an impressionist painter, Billy can musically create an aura of restlessness and a desparate need to move. The unfulfilled woman tried for years to make good a bad marriage; finally

*"all those stories of the good life
convinced her not to hang around."*

She's California bound, with the requisite stop in Nevada en route for a quickie divorce.

With lush string backing and a female choir, the woman's journey assumes an added dimension of drama that increases the effectiveness of the song. Part of Billy's vocal delivery is slightly mournful;

he is nicely sympathetic with the woman's plight. It is also worth noting that this is the first song on the album that seems to be not at all about him. Yet a good bit of emotional involvement remains in his performance.

We've noticed before, in "The Ballad of Billy The Kid" for example, that Joel sometimes will sneak in a line or two when we're least expecting it, startling us a bit by changing the subject without a warning. In "Stop In Nevada," there is a line that says,

"and though he never tried to make her she often thought it would be nice."

Who are we talking about all of the sudden? Certainly not the husband; who is this guy who never reappears in the song? Adultery does not seem a motive for her departure. However, Joel has let us know that this is a contemplative woman with a lot more on her mind than anyone seems to know. Perhaps this is one of those fleeting thoughts that grabs hold for a spell.

"If I Only Had The Words (To Tell You)" is pure pop, not a rocker at all. It demonstrates Billy's debt to popular songwriters of a different age. It also corroborates one critic's mention of Billy Joel and Anthony Newley in the same breath. The vocally flexible Joel sounds very much like Newley on this track.

Along with "Ain't No Crime," this is one of the duds on *Piano Man*. A relationship is floundering, and the singer is frustrated that he can't verbalize whatever might save it. He's explaining all of this with his role as a musician very much in mind; among other things, he's miffed that the radio plays a lot of lines he might have used.

Unfortunately, "If I Only Had The Words" is very bland from a musical standpoint and all too obvious and mundane from a lyrical one. Lines like

Wide World Photos

Michael Putland/Retna

*"but I only have these arms to hold you
and that's all that you can ask
of any man"*

are hardly groundbreaking, and hardly worthy of a man who has shown himself to be a sharp wordsmith many times on this album. Detractors could point to this song to say that Billy Joel is nothing special. What they should do is just skip this song and advance to his better material.

In "Somewhere Along The Line," Billy, with a full belly, is enjoying a rainy night in Paris while realizing that

*"tomorrow there'll be hell to pay
somewhere along the line."*

The entire song is about life as an enjoy-now, pay-later proposition. The postprandial cigarettes he's savoring will eventually destroy his lungs, the rent will come due. Even the wonderful relationship he has put together will in some way take its toll. "You pay for your satisfaction" is the lesson he's learned. And as he sits in the Paris cafe in the prime of life, with a guitar crying behind him, young Billy notes that "a young man is the king of every kingdom that he sees." Alas, "there's an old and feeble man not far behind," and that man is also him.

Electric guitar provides the musical framework for the song, punctuating it at the beginning and closing it off at the end. The production is suitably bombastic, and Billy provides some telling rock-piano riffs. He has mainly been playing acoustic piano throughout, often in the midst of many other instruments, but he has managed to stand out without electrically amplifying his keyboard. "Somewhere Along The Line" has a striking arrangement and a sobering message, effectively conveyed by Joel and his ensemble.

The capper on the *Piano Man* album is "Captain Jack," deservedly an FM favorite and the first song to make Billy Joel anything close to a household word. The presence of Rhys Clark on drums (Ron Tutt drummed on all the other *Piano Man* tracks) provides a link to the days of *Cold Spring Harbor,* on which Clark was featured.

At 6:55, "Captain Jack" is easily the record's lengthiest number, and it is an ambitious and mammoth undertaking. Much of Joel's reputation for sardonicism and biting social commentary, often directed at suburban lifestyles, found its origins in "Captain Jack." It is unrelenting and pretty nasty. As he sings "Captain Jack," disdain seems to be Billy Joel's major motivator.

The first few notes seem well off in the distance, muted, almost like bagpipes on the vast and eerie moors of Scotland. But Billy, as he often does with his lyrics, quickly establishes the place, the time, the character, and the mood. It's there in the first couplet:

*"Saturday night and you're still hangin'
  around
Tired of livin' in your one-horse town."*

It's boring suburbia, where the kid's only escape is to "go to the village in your tie-dyed jeans" and voyeuristically view the freaks. What might be a dream for some—split-level life on the outer fringes of the metropolis—is, in "Captain Jack," painted as the most dismal, bleak, and useless of existences.

The poor slob—a twenty-one-year-old suburban lad—gets the details of his dreary lot thrown in his face by Billy. His sister's got a Saturday night date, but he has to "sit at home and masturbate," a degrading way of satisfying the same need, for sure. This, by the way, may have been the first direct mention of self-abuse ever to go over the FM airwaves.

Between the verses comes the repeated and reassuring chorus:

*"Captain Jack will get you high tonight
And take you to your special island."*

It is never made any clearer exactly who or what Captain Jack is, but that's not important. Indeed, it is better that he/it remain undefined and therefore universally applicable. Captain Jack is whoever or whatever this twenty-one-year-old needs to get him to the state of consciousness that will at least temporarily blot out his miseries. Clearly, the possibility that it is a drug is very much there, but it needn't necessarily be that. As a salve to all sorts of youthful anxieties, Captain Jack is a seventies counterpart to Mr. Tambourine Man.

Still, whatever relief Captain Jack brings is all too impermanent. In rather scornful tones, Billy begins to show us that our young suburbanite is a pathetic sort who can't win for losing. He's the kind of guy who can stand on a streetcorner looking spiffy in a new English outfit and, as Billy tells us, you know any minute he's going to be picking his nose.

Things go from bad to worse, from ineptness to genuine disaster.

*"They just found your father in the swimming pool
And you guess you won't be going back to school."*

Captain Jack may get him high tonight, but this kid is beginning to get some rather strong doses of adversity from his biographer Billy.

The guy seeks relief by listening to his records, smoking pot, and parking with his girl, but Billy reminds him,

*"still you're aching for the things you haven't got
What went wrong?"*

The schlep is getting nowhere fast.

*"you're 21 and still your mother makes you're bed
and that's too long,"*

notes Billy, who begins to feel freer to make value judgements as the evidence mounts against his subject.

By this time, this lad's life truly seems damned, but the final chords of the song still celebrate the all-curing power of Captain Jack. At this point, perhaps, Joel is being more than a bit tongue-in-cheek. The guy he's writing about can use any escape mechanism he chooses to forget his predicament, but he's still in the midst of that predicament and making no progress.

The music of "Captain Jack" alternates a rather simple tune in the verses, highlighted by piano underpinnings from Billy, with the very majestic "Captain Jack will get you high tonight" choruses. The choruses feature somewhat celestial organ from Billy and swirling Boleroesque guitar phrases. At the end, with Joel now singing in impassioned fashion, the guitarist is climbing higher and higher, perhaps in an effort to transcend these suburban realms once and for all. This is a truly rousing instrumental finale, imbuing this suburban saga with a sense of gradeur that is strikingly antithetical to its theme. Of course, the more antithetical the better, in this case.

Joel's distaste for suburban blandness is well publicized and quite justifiable for a songwriter who has experienced Levittown firsthand. As far as spitting on its subject is concerned, "Captain Jack" is right up there with Bob Dylan's "Ballad of a Thin Man" and John Lennon's "Working Class Hero." "Captain Jack" *is* electrifying. A direct frontal assault lyrically and an epic musically, it is intended to startle and it does. It is not surprising that it had such an impact early on, and it would naturally get frequent airplay from disc jockeys who shared Joel's distaste for vanilla lifestyles.

An irony of all this, of course, is that much of Billy's audience consists of exactly the kind of young people he's talking about. They do the things he's writing about; they go into the Village in New York and gawk at the natives. They do live in their parents' houses, sequestering themselves in the shelter of their one room, hardly expanding their horizons. A kick in the ass wouldn't hurt them one bit. If "Captain Jack" provided that, it performed a public service.

For a debut album on a major label, *Piano Man* was rather ambitious in scope. The material was strong enough to form a lasting impression of Billy Joel in the mind; depending on what songs a listener focused on, that impression would vary. "Piano Man" would suggest that Billy is a consummate entertainer and showman prone to autobiography; in other words, that he *is* the piano man. Lovers of romantic ballads had a basis for putting Billy in the romantic balladeer category, although his best work in that genre was yet to come. To "Captain Jack" fans he was a pungent, acerbic critic of aspects of his own culture, and one who pulled no punches. To a few, unfortunately, he came to be thought of as a suburban songwriter; these people clearly ignored the meaning of Joel's words.

Piano Man has plenty of excellent material and fine performances. Billy's songwriting, singing, and playing capacities were obviously blossoming.

Piano Man was one of the more striking debuts of 1973 and showed Billy Joel to be a solo artist of high caliber. There were rough edges to be smoothed out, but his songwriting prowess was particularly impressive. Columbia seemed to have a major talent on its hands.

Maureen Orth of *Newsweek,* in a 1974 article on Billy and another Long

Billy Joel and Dave Brubeck at Puerto Rican Festival.

Chuck Pulin

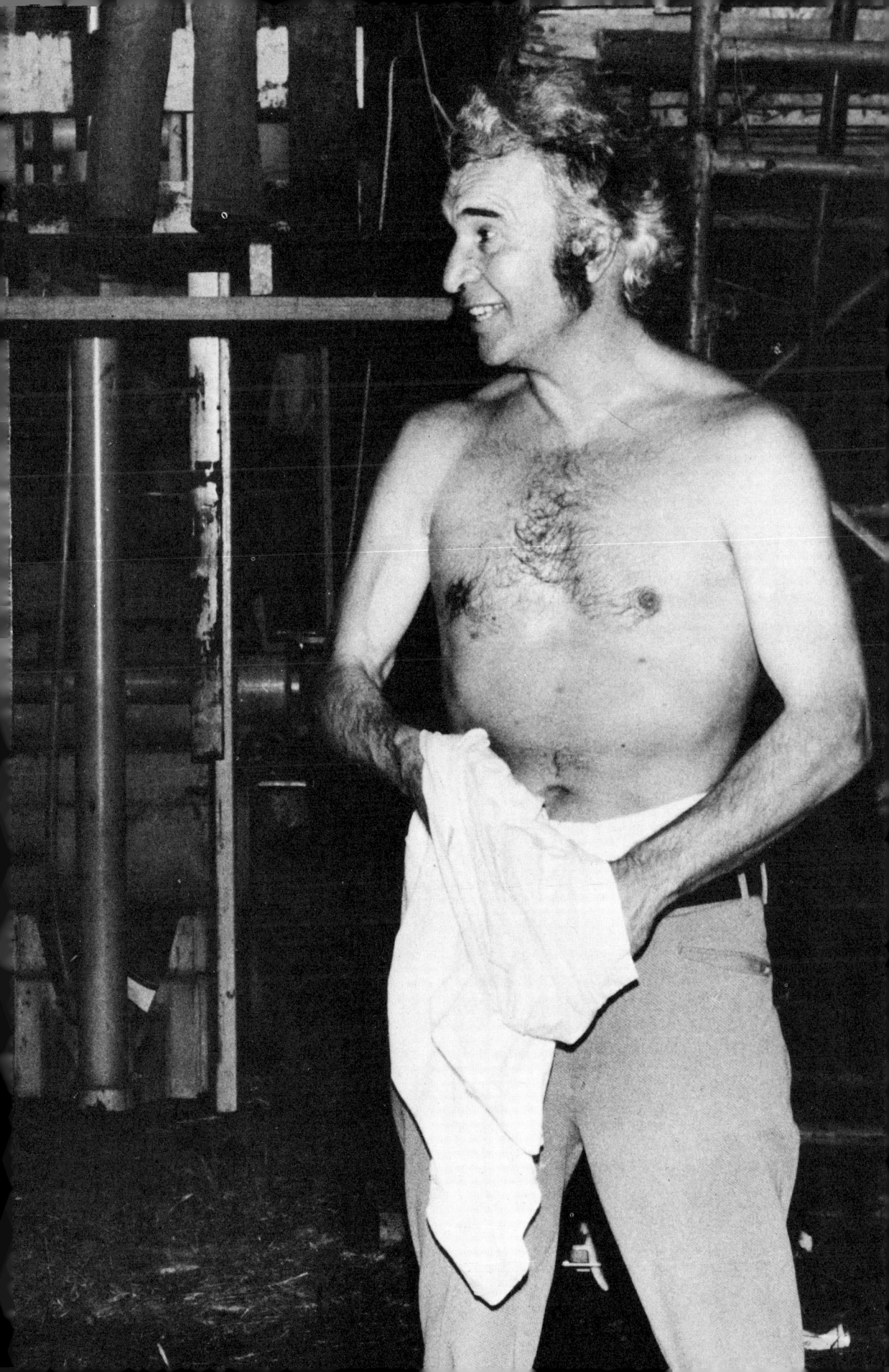

Island singer-songwriter, Elliott Murphy, contended that both men were dealing with "middle-class blues—the dull monotony of growing up where your consciousness is defined by the perimeters of the shopping-center parking lot." Orth suggested that suburban kids were "finding pain in those split-levels." Murphy, in fact, called suburbia "a terminal case of boredom."

Billy was living in Oyster Bay, L.I. when he wrote "Captain Jack;" that would explain the Oyster Bay reference in "The Ballad of Billy The Kid."

"Captain Jack" was penned "when being a druggie was in full flower," he told Orth. "I was kind of down on my own peer group. I can understand but not condone somebody in the ghetto shooting up. What I can't understand is why kids from Long Island should."

Much has been made of supposed similarities between Billy Joel and Harry Chapin—too much, probably. There are indications that Joel isn't too pleased with the comparison. In fact, other musicians react negatively to a comparison with Chapin. Meat Loaf once commented in print that he would become violent the next time someone said their singing voices were similar.

The Joel-Chapin comparison comes about for a few evident reasons. Both have roots in suburbia. Despite attempts they may make to be soulful, they are both obviously *very* white musicians. And they spin long, involved yarns about just plain folks.

But the differences are more important than the similarities. Although both men often write very pointed lyrics, Chapin, even in comparison to Joel, has about as much subtlety as a bludgeon. Billy Joel by his own admission is above all else a musician, and he always remains musical; Chapin is more of a balladeer who has resorted to the musical idiom for convenience sake. And Billy Joel rocks with reckless abandon a good percentage of the time; if Chapin does so at all, he does it quite rarely. Joel has moved his milieu to the city; while Chapin's subjects may occasionally be urban, the sound never is. Finally, Billy Joel is obviously reaching his peak as a songwriter; Harry Chapin hasn't written a memorable tune in years. If there was ever a common ground that they had mutually staked out, Billy Joel clearly dominates it now.

Michael Putland/Retna

CHAPTER 3

"Streetlife Serenade"

Michael Putland/Retna

Streetlife Serenade, the 1974 Billy Joel release, was, like its predecessor, recorded at Devonshire and produced by Michael Stewart. This time out, Joel shared an arranging credit with Stewart.

Part of the cast of *Piano Man* is back, including drummer Ron Tutt and bassists Emory Gordy and Wilton Felder. The bass chores are also shared by master sessionman Larry Knechtel, who had appeared on *Cold Spring Harbor* and was now a bit of a star in his own, thanks to his membership in Bread. The country touches—pedal steel and banjo—were supplied by Tom Whitehorse, with Joe Clayton on conga and William Smith on organ.

If there was a schizophrenic quality to *Streetlife Serenade,* a problem in establishing a group sound with an individual brand, it might be partially because the guitar spot on the album seemed almost to belong to whoever was in the neighborhood at the time. No fewer than eight guitarists are featured; Richard Bennett from *Piano Man,* plus Gary Dalton, Mike Deasy, Roj Rathor, Al Hertzberg, Don Evans, Art Munson, and Michael Stewart himself.

Brian Hagiwara's cover painting for *Streetlife Serenade* captures, in very broad strokes, the curbside feeling of Anytown, U.S.A. The back-cover photo by Jim Marshall depicts Billy in soft focus. Wearing a flannel shirt and jeans, barefoot and straddling a wicker chair, he looks a bit menacing. Whether he was

consciously playing up his reputed pugnaciousness or just letting it be known that he is uncomfortable about posing for pictures is known perhaps only to him.

Streetlife Serenade came out fairly soon after *Piano Man,* considering the fact that both are entirely self-written albums. Although Joel is *prolific* and was spending much of his time sequestered for songwriting purposes during this period, he probably didn't have as much strong material as he should have had. He has stated in print that the second album can never be as good as the first; obviously you don't hold back your best material when you're making a debut record. Nevertheless, there is that matter of momentum to consider; Joel had done well with *Piano Man,* but he was not yet the kind of artist who could expect that hundreds of thousands of people would automatically purchase whatever he put out.

The second Columbia LP has a few standout tracks, more that are merely fair to middling, and a few that qualify as failures. It has begun to sell well now that Billy's popularity is affecting his entire catalogue, but *Streetlife Serenade* is quite clearly his weakest Columbia album. Still and all, it is *not* a bad album.

The first song, "Streetlife Serenader," has a dissonant piano intro that launches us into the rather elegiac mood of this selection. There are problems with this one. Most of the lyrics are not grammatical sentences but a string of adjective-noun combinations ("Child of Eisenhower/New World Celebrator"). Despite these gobs of information, we miss an overall picture—like, for instance, what is the real point of this song? We know that this streetlife serenader performs to his utmost and barely scratches out a living—that's in there somewhere—but the actual thesis here seems to be absent.

"Streetlife Serenader" runs 5:18, and the material can't support such a time span. Billy's piano chords are appropriately mournful, but he could use a bit more support, perhaps from a second lead instrument. And his singing comes across with great feeling, although in some spots he substitutes emotion for articulation. For an opening, number, this is pretty thin stuff.

"Los Angelenos," on the other hand, is pungent social commentary on the lifestyles the recent California transplant has observed. Droll California commentary had been the forte of distinguished men of letters like Evelyn Waugh and Aldous Huxley, so why shouldn't Billy Joel get into the act?

The music is tough and aggressive, propelled by organ, guitar, and thumping bass. Billy gets right to the point:

*"Los Angelenos all come from somewhere
to live in sunshine, their funky exile."*

People wander to L.A. and apparently continue to wander in search of real or imagined exotic lifestyles. Many of them are "going nowhere on the streets with the Spanish names." Life consists of being perpetually on the make; the young girls are mature beyond their years. It seems "all so easy to become acquainted."

Joel knows what it all means, however. After several of the verses stating the various high falutin' activities of the Angelenos, Billy remarks that what they're really doing is "making up for all the time gone by." There seems to be a prevalent Ben Gazzara-type "Run For Your Life" mentality—you remember, squeeze twenty years of living into one, or maybe two. Time waits for no man, but time doesn't *always* move at such a breakneck pace.

"Los Angelenos" reflects the ambivalence of a young man still stunned by much of what he sees. He is attracted and appalled at the same instant. But he has grasped many of life's realities and successfully fitted them into the framework of a song. About the only criticism one should have of "Los Angelenos," and it's a minor one, is that Ron Tutt's drums are mixed too high.

"The Great Suburban Showdown" begins a bit like a modern death dance. Actually, the opening is very reminiscent of "Slaughter on Tenth Avenue." There is a suggestion in the title, and it is sustained by the lyrics, that what is about to occur is every bit as grim as the fateful gunfight at the O.K. Corral. Actually, many adolescents and young adults listening to "The Great Suburban Showdown" would agree with Billy that returning to one's boyhood home is even *more* frightening.

En route from somewhere by plane, the singer, contemplating the inevitable, laments, "guess I saw this coming down the line," as if it were as obvious as death and taxes.

The horrifying ritual is revealed:

*"sit around with the folks
tell the same old tired jokes
bored to death on Sunday afternoon."*

Sunday means football, church, or a day of rest to some people, but to a lot of them like Billy, this is precisely what Sunday means. The only solution isn't even a very tasty one; it is to hide, as the singer does, in his room—even if it hasn't been his room for several years.

*"I've been gone for a while
made some changes in my style."*

observes the singer, and that is the sad truth. People grow, but certain situations remain stagnant. Some people enjoy nostalgia, some find security in the familiar, but others prefer to keep things current. The latter group includes those who believe there is nothing worse than getting sucked back into one's past.

The tune of "The Great Suburban Showdown" is quite light; it needn't be any more overpowering, since the lyrics deftly tell the whole story. After the "Slaughter on Tenth Avenue" intro, in fact, one begins to pick up vague tracks of a country flavor. If the suburbs Billy had been talking about were on the edge of Nashville, he might have had a shot at the country charts.

"Showdown" is obviously an addition to Billy's portfolio as suburban chronicler, but the approach here is quite different from that of, say, "Captain Jack." That song was an out-and-out attack; no empathy was shared. On "The Great Suburban Showdown," however, the protagonist is feeling the pain of re-encountering wretched blandness, and he is expressing it in such a wide-open manner as to invite plenty of "you ain't kidding, that's just how it is" responses. Here, Billy Joel gets a response from way down deep; that's certainly a measure of success.

"Root Beer Rag" is just a brief piece of barrel-house piano by Billy. It isn't ragtime, however; it sounds a lot like the stuff they were playing on those steam-powered calliopes that were in circulation during the Bicentennial. It also contains a few piano passages that were to turn up in later Billy Joel songs. Basically, "Root Beer Rag" is an opportunity to show that Joel has quick fingers and can control them. Drummer Ron Tutt keeps pace all along the way. "Root Beer Rag" is supposed to be a bit of fun and whimsy and an interlude, but it is not particularly nourishing to the ear. It's okay but it's trivial, much flimsier than "Nocturne" on *Cold Spring Harbor.*

"Roberta" is the final cut on the first side of *Streetlife Serenade.* It might appear to be a simple devotional from one man to one woman, but there's more beneath the surfaces. This is R-rated stuff; Roberta would appear to be a rather expensive call girl with whom Billy is smitten.

*"You say you know me
but I see only what you're paid to show me."*

The insouciance of Billy's vocal delivery (and once again, a bit of Anthony Newley creeps in) is in direct contrast to the rather desperate intent of the lyrics. "Roberta, how I've adored you / I'd ask you over but I can't afford you," admits the singer, who cannot keep her in the style to which she is accustomed. By song's end his needs are more acute, and he is not coy: "I'm in a bad way and I wanna make love to you . . . I really need you, but I suppose my small change won't see you through."

"Roberta" is the kind of song one might let slip by without a close listen. But it is really remarkable. It is the only seventies popular song that comes to mind about a man's devotion to a particular prostitute, and certainly the only one that is offered up in such a hallowed framework. Several times throughout the song, Billy is joined by a backing chorus that is so celestial it seems to be singing hosannas. Billy's dedication to Roberta is almost religious. Juxtaposed with so secular a subject, the sacred treatment is quite amusing. This isn't exactly subtlety, but "Roberta" shows that Billy Joel is capable of marvelous irony, something we hadn't previously seen a great deal of in his compositions.

Side two begins with "The Entertainer," the best-known and most often heard song on *Streetlife Serenade.* It's kind of "Piano Man Part II." While "Piano Man" was a slice of what life as a lounge performer of modest reputation entailed, "The Entertainer" offers us that same fellow a short while later, after he's begun to make it in the recording business. Since many folks (particularly AM audiences) knew Billy first on the basis of "Piano Man" and "The Entertainer," it is not surprising that he gained a reputation as chiefly an autobiographer.

Musically, "Piano Man" and "The Entertainer" have nothing in common. "Piano Man" was representative of soft, sedate lounge fare. By comparison, "The Entertainer" is very swift, and it rocks, and the latter song also has big role for the moog synthesizer to play.

Billy, who works fast when he works best, reportedly wrote fifteen verses of "The Entertainer" while watching "The Midnight Special."

Joel's aggressive stance on "The Entertainer" is that of a man who in his profession can state, "I know just where I stand." The road from "Piano Man" to "The Entertainer" has been a rocky one, with plenty of lessons learned along the way.

This may be the strongest lyric on *Streetlife Serenade.* Considering how quickly the song moves along, and how many truisms he tries to pack into the verses, it is amazing how Billy has managed to fit his message so masterfully into a regular metric scheme. It doesn't hurt, either, that his bravado vocal doesn't miss a step.

There are so many striking lines in "The Entertainer" that it is difficult to pinpoint the most telling. Joel appreciates his degree of fame but understands how short-lived it can be; he may be today's champion, but "I won't be here in another year if I don't stay on the charts."

Almost inevitably, mistakes have to be made, many of the business variety: "things I did not know at first I learned by doing twice." And there are the people who have pieces to take away: "still they come to haunt me, still they have their say . . . so I rub my neck and

Michael Putland/Retna

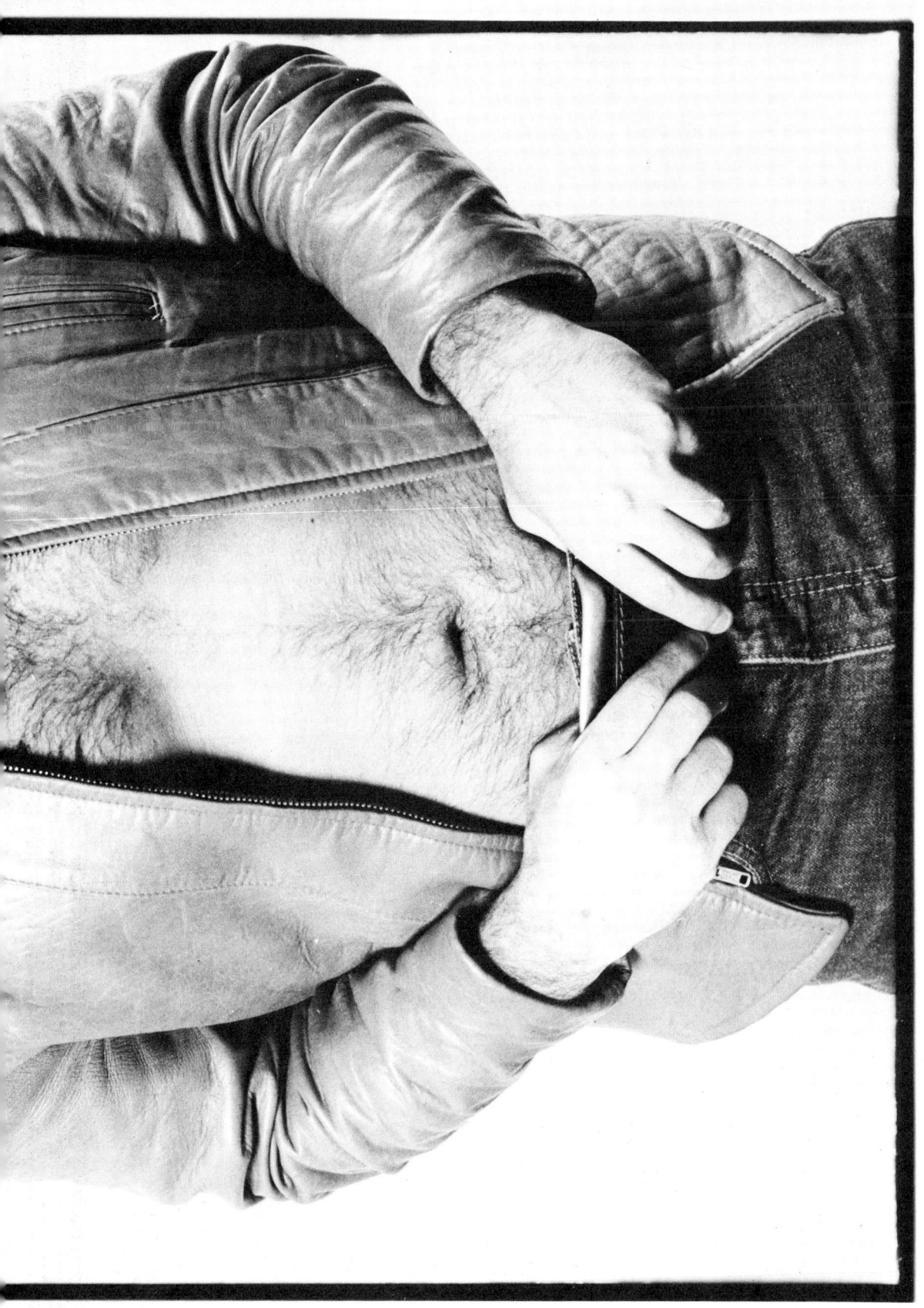

I write 'em a check and they go their merry way."

From a musical standpoint, "The Entertainer" may be the album's most expertly structured track. There are no show solos; the job here is to keep things moving, and a sort of layering occurs. There is Billy's piano, punctuating with its staccato style, never unnecessarily florid. There is a regularly rhythmic acoustic next, which is later abetted by Tom Whitehorse's banjo; of all essentially piano-based singer-songwriters, Billy Joel seems to find more use for banjo than anyone else. Finally, there is Billy's moog synthesizer, with its spacy quality, that provides the "bookends" at the beginning and end.

Entertainer Billy is much-traveled but somewhat world-weary. The complaints sound very much like those that would dominate Jackson Browne's *Running On Empty* album several years later. Joel has stayed in the so-called best places, squired all sorts of lovely women, but isn't too good at remembering names or faces: "after a while and a thousand miles it all becomes the same." He'd like to hang around a bit longer sometimes, but neither the schedule nor expenses will permit it.

Perhaps the saddest reality Billy faces in "The Entertainer" is the commercial reality. Like other musical talents who care a lot about the artistic end of what they do, he has complained in the past about the pressure to create a hit single. As he says here, he can create something he is truly proud of, something that required "the best years of my life," and who will know? "If you wanna have a hit you gotta make it fit, so they cut it down to 3:05."

Like it or not—and this song stresses the dislikes—what reoccurs is the notion that performing lives are very mortal. And the ultimate sobering thought is, no matter what kind of well-publicized idol he may be today, "I won't be here in another year if I don't stay on the charts."

And that's the final word. A truer picture of the dark side of pop stardom probably hasn't been written, although in the years since there have been many such attempts, including those by the aforementioned Browne. Billy Joel is never vague; he always takes a definite point of view. Here, with "The Entertainer," he has come up with the definitive song on the subject.

"In 'The Entertainer,' I was saying 'Don't make gods out of us. Appreciate us for our humanity,' " Joel revealed to Timothy White. "I'm not caught up in that 'stardom' lie. It's a ball of gas."

"Last Of The Big Time Spenders" is a quiet followup to the fury of "The Entertainer." It is also not very memorable. Instrumentally thin, it might be part of the basis of Billy's complaint that he's really wanted more guitar on *Streetlife Serenade*. His piano and the rhythm section are mixed high, however; because of that, and the tendency Billy still had at that time to ennunciate less when he opted for soulfulness, his meaning at times is lost.

Like "Roberta," "Last Of The Big Time Spenders" is about a suitor who is woefully short of finances. The title is actually a play on the original meaning of the phrase; here, time is all Billy has to spend.

"If time is an indication of the wealth that I never knew
then I'm the last of the big time spenders
'cause I've been spending time on you"

declares the man who wonders how he's going to handle the next rent check.

Again, the country edges crop up in the music of Joel, who is definitely not a country boy. But Billy seems to understand that pedal-steel guitar is the musical instrument most capable of expressing a sigh, and this is one of several songs in which the situation calls for one long sigh. Still, beyond Tom Whitehorse's pedal-steel work, the arrangement is a bit tepid. And once you get the little joke in the title, there's not much more here to hold your attention.

Here, on side two, we begin to get indications that first-rate material for *Streetlife Serenade* was in short supply. "Weekend Song" sounds, unfortunately, like filler. The protagonist here has worked nine-to-five for the same company for seven years and has not amassed a fortune; hmm, financial straits seem to be a recurring theme on this album. He can't afford a vacation, but he can afford to take the train out to his home (in the suburbs?) and spend some Friday night money on his date.

It would be too much to call this a bad song; it isn't painful to listen to or anything. But the story is old and familiar, and the music is unremarkable. It is an upbeat tune, and the balance of the individual vocalists and instruments could have been a bit clearer. A guitar is featured in the beginning and in a solo somewhere near the midpoint, but the playing is merely workmanship, far short of dazzling.

That makes two weak links in a row. The next offering, "Souvenir," is better; it is nice, but it is rather slight and won't bowl anybody over in 2:01. "Souvenir" would serve nicely as an interlude after a very strong piece of material, but it doesn't follow anything strong.

"Souvenir" features a sadly reflective Billy at the piano, chronicling the tangible reminiscences of someone's past—the post cards, the programs, the photographs. Not a joyful theme here—the notion is that life "slowly fades away." And souvenirs give merely fleeting consolation:

Jeffrey Mayer

*"your mementos will turn to dust
but that's the price you pay."*

Billy has tackled a number of subjects on *Streetlife Serenade,* so why not try mortality, even if it doesn't seem to fit into the overall scheme (is there one?). "Souvenir" is a mere tidbit, inoffensive, a lyrical denouement to the album (although one instrumental track follows). Bidding us soft adieu is okay, but it would have been better if heftier material were etched in our memories.

That problem is alleviated somewhat by the instrumental finale, "The Mexican Connection." Again a certain obsession with the West is apparent. The brief piano opening, done near the very bottom of those eighty-eights, sounds like "Catch A Falling Star" Latin-style, but much of the body of the tune brings to mind the theme from *The Magnificent Seven* or the music from the Marlboro commercials. There is a whole slew of keyboards at work here—piano, organ, and moog, at least—but never in combat, more in alternation. But the emotionally uplifting melody, conjuring up a taste of those wide-open spaces, is carried by a guitarist whose twanginess is very much in the manner of Al Caiola, the guy who used to play on all those Western movies and TV soundtracks. "The Mexican Connection" is smoothly and sweetly performed. It lasts 3:38 but has a certain timeless quality; if it had gone on five times as long it probably would have felt just the same.

If you listen to *Streetlife Serenade* late at night, or with a certain yearning for a spell in the wilderness, "The Mexican Connection" will send you away restfully and happily.

Still, it doesn't obscure the fact that while *Streetlife Serenade* is nothing to get angry about, most of it is quite forgettable. Few of its songs have become staples of Joel's repertoire, few are requested, and few get radio airplay today.

An opportunity to capitalize on the popularity of *Piano Man* seems to have been missed; perhaps more time was needed, or perhaps more control by the artist himself.

In his 1977 *High Fidelity* interview (it ran in '78), Joel made derogatory comments about *Piano Man* and *Streetlife Serenade.* "There's something very mushy and powderpuffy about them," he charged. "I like to rock & roll."

Chuck Pulin

CHAPTER 4

Back to New York

On the basis of the continued success of *Piano Man* in the earlier part of 1974, Billy Joel won *Cashbox* magazine's award as "Best New Male Vocalist" for that year. Most importantly, Billy was graduating to the role of headliner on the road and was selling out prestige places like Carnegie Hall and Lincoln Center in New York; Kiel Opera House in St. Louis; and Massey Hall in Toronto.

After *Streetlife Serenade* Billy was to part company with his producer. "I got along good with Michael Stewart," he explained later to Dave Marsh. "I got a lot of empathy for Michael Stewart. He was under a lot of pressure. The only time we ran into a problem was when it came down to, I had a band together that had been on the road for two years and he didn't want to use them on the recordings. That's when I parted ways with Michael Stewart."

There were also apparent differences in the studio. "The producer had in his mind what he wanted to hear, he wanted technical perfection. I didn't know shit. I was writing songs on the piano, but I wrote sometimes, 'This is a guitar song'. But the producer had in his head, 'Okay, Billy Joel plays piano, so we bring out the piano. Never mind the rock & roll part of it. We gotta feature Billy Joel'. It was like pulling teeth in the studio."

Another change he elected to make was geographical. "When the New York financial crisis started happening, there

Retna

was a lot of anti-New York sentiment in L.A. from former New Yorkers and I got pissed off," he stated. "I woke up one day and just said, 'I'm going back.'" In fact, his return was to the upstate New York community of Highland Falls. It was there that he penned most of the material for *Turnstiles*.

"I lived in California three years; I still like California, the West Coast in general. The weather is nice, the native California people are nice, the rent was cheap," he explained to Dave Marsh. "When I needed it, it was there. I didn't go out there with the intention of staying. I just went there to try to get my business affairs straightened out."

Turnstiles was a long time getting off the ground. James Guercio, who produced several bestsellers for Chicago, began to work with Billy. Guercio wanted to use drummer Nigel Olsson and bassist Dee Murray, both part of Elton John's band, but Billy wanted his own guys. Still, he tried that line-up for two months, without satisfactory results.

Guercio and Joel next went to New York and A&R studios to record with session players there, and still things weren't gelling. Ultimately, Billy split to Long Island with his own guys, went into Ultrasonic studios, and produced *Turnstiles* himself. "I had my own band," he explained later. "They knew it cold."

For the *Turnstiles* sessions at Ultrasonic in Hempstead, producer Joel brought in John Bradley as engineer and production supervisor. Musician Joel had Doug Stegmeyer and Liberty DeVitto as bassist and drummer on every track. The guitar cast was reduced to three; Howie Emerson, Russell Javors, and James Smith were all making their first recorded appearances with Billy Joel. On some tracks, Richie Cannata was brought in on saxophone and Mingo Lewis was an additional percussionist. Ken Ascher's orchestral arrangements were added at Colum-

Ken Regan/Camera 5

bia Recordings Studios in New York City. Necessary overdubs were done at Jim Guercio's Caribou Recording Studios in Colorado.

If *Turnstiles,* among other things, is Billy Joel's way of saying "hello, I'm back" to his friends and fans in the East, the album-cover art surely shows that. In shirtsleeves and loosely knotted tie, Billy stands before a gathering of folks on a subway platform. Those assembled, photographed by Jerry Abramowitz, are nicely representative metropolitan types. There's a glamorous couple, including a platinum blond, gaily out for a night on the town. There's a dour grandmother and her equally solemn grandson, a young woman smiling beneath the stereo headset that drowns out the clamor of the subway, and a proper young exec or grad student, laden with the book that will undoubtedly accelerate his advance to the top.

Turnstiles is such an enormous improvement over *Streetlife Serenade* that one would almost imagine Joel had emerged from some prolonged semi-comatose state. It is still primarily a songwriter's album; the emphasis is chiefly on words and basic melody, not the fully developed sound that would be heard on later albums.

That approach is fine, however, because the material Joel put together for *Turnstiles* is truly topnotch. Some of these songs are well on their way to becoming contemporary standards. And if *Turnstiles* still did not restore Billy to the commercial popularity of *Piano Man*, it was fresh evidence that he was a gifted talent of major proportions. Singers looking for songs to cover, and other people in the music business, took note of the genius at work on *Turnstiles,* and that, in the long run, was the significance of the album to Joel's career.

The public, meanwhile, could take heart in the fact that *Turnstiles* was the first Billy Joel record on which there wasn't a single weak number. Every track here was worthy of inclusion. Very few records have that distinction.

Turnstiles in part chronicles Billy's exodus from California and his return to his native New York. His impressions of both places, and the reasons for his move, provide the substance of many of the Joel compositions here.

"Say Goodbye To Hollywood," along with being an obvious farewell to his temporarily adopted homeland, is an homage to Phil Spector and his production techniques. The beginning, with its thumping bass drum and tambourine, could be straight out of "Be My Baby." Some of the other Spector elements are here as well—the solid bass and piano foundation, the clicks that sound like castanets. The string orchestration by Ken Ascher is lush but not excessive, just the way it was on all those early sixties hits.

The drumming of Liberty DeVitto might seem a little heavy-limbed and too concentrated on the cymbals, but that's precisely how it should be in a Spector tribute. Richie Cannata, making his first appearance with Joel, supplies a sax solo that is bona fide fifties and sixties rock & roll. It is deep and rich, with not a note wasted.

In fact, for a production that involves so many elements, Joel accomplished something rather extraordinary by not overdoing or wasting anything, not making anything sound out of place. Of particular interest is where he has placed his vocal in the midst of this "wall of sound." He doesn't soar over it; he's smack dab in the middle, even occasionally behind it a bit, like a distant peal, or like someone in transit still moving toward his objective. The singing is a bit restrained, especially in comparison with a later and very famous cover version of this song, but the author's own interpretation is both legitimate and appropriate. This is a substantial and sophisticated enough song to warrant several interpretations.

Parts of the theme of "Say Goodbye To Hollywood" are also vintage Spector; his protagonists were also the young and the restless. *Turnstiles* is the first Billy Joel album on which the listener is provided with printed lyrics; if that's an expression of confidence in the material, there are ample grounds for it. The saga of hero Bobby here is one of many gripping tales.

Young Bobby, in a spiffy rented car, runs the lights as he races to join the nighttime scene on Sunset Boulevard; Billy Joel tells us all of this in the first two lines.

Bobby is one of the colorful characters that people the Hollywood Billy Joel knew; Johnny, whose "style is so right for troubadours," is another. Yet the dilemma he writes of here is the one that the author faced in his own life; one can cite many positive reasons for staying in one place, but other stronger factors can at the same time dictate a need to move on.

Joel had his first real tastes of fame and (modest) fortune in California, but for sanity and creativity's sake it became necessary to pack up and leave. It did not have to happen with bitterness; this farewell to Hollywood contains no anger. The decision is just a delicate one that comes after weighing the pros and cons and deciding what's best for oneself. What he says about it has the weight of a truism: "Moving on is a chance that you take every time you try to stay together."

The final glance back is resigned but wistful:

*"So many faces in and out of my life
Some will last, some will just be now and then."*

Ain't it the truth—and it's the truth brilliantly told and capably set in a Spectorish framework. "Say Goodbye To Hollywood" is the strongest leadoff track on any of Joel's first three Columbia albums, and it has a universality that attracts so many other recording artists to it.

"Summer, Highland Falls" is a title which evokes the time and place where many of the *Turnstiles* tunes were written. It is a time for taking stock of oneself; as Joel suggest, "there is a time for meditation in cathedrals of our own."

Much of "Summer, Highland Falls" is virtually a piano solo for Billy, and the music is a series of arpeggios, with the first note of each sequence played off the beat. The effect is that of flight and motion; specifically, of the author watching the events of his recent life and trying to give a meaning to them. Here is some of the finest piano work on the album.

"Summer, Highland Falls" is largely about love and relationships, a relationship that isn't quite as trouble-free as the author would like to have imagined. It is not, however, one that is on the skids; it's definitely strong enough to try to straighten out and save. The lovers may not be ideal fantasy figures to each other, but they have experiences in common, they often arrive mentally at the same place. There is also the pain of seeing a loved one feeling downtrodden. Billy says it well:

*"Now I have seen that sad surrender in my lover's eyes
And I can only stand apart and sympathize."*

Helplessness can be one of the most miserable feelings known to man and woman.

"All You Wanna Do Is Dance" is the lightest tune on *Turnstiles,* and it is fun and well done. The beat is a variation of reggae, the first such undertaking for Billy Joel. Stegmeyer is particularly good here, with his bass rhythms giving the song much of its sprightliness.

In "All You Wanna Do Is Dance," Billy is frustrated with his lover's continuing fascination with the past. It is, however, a patient form of frustration; he does not sound peeved.

The woman is a child of the sixties cast adrift in the seventies, the kind who still wants to know when the Beatles are getting back together. "You wish you were back in the good old days, when tomatoes were cheaper," Billy admonishes her gently; those were also the days when "you didn't get any (unless you went steady and made out for a year)."

These aren't earth-shattering problems; she'll eventually grow out of her obsession with the past, but Billy would like to see it soon.

*"You want to crawl back into yesterday
You don't want to deal with the future,"*

he tells her. Apparently, all she wants to do is dance her days away.

There's a basic lesson very mildly told here; we'd best all get on with it and not keep looking back. Written when the nostalgia boom was already in full bloom, "All You Wanna Do Is Dance" may be expressing Joel's irritation with that phenomenon.

In any case, this is a nice number, very different from anything else Billy has ever done. In the breaks between the verses, someone is playing steel piano like a true master; for a while, you're transported to a colorful Caribbean street festival.

On the next song, you are back in the very real world of the Empire State on "New York State Of Mind," but to Billy that is a very welcome state of consciousness. With the possible exception of "Piano Man," this is Joel's best-known song before the halcyon days of *The Stranger* and *52nd Street*. It is also a theme song for everyone who has any reason at all to love New York; so many specific glories of the place are itemized that there's a line in here for just about anyone.

As part of the album *Turnstiles,* which marks his return to New York, "New York State Of Mind" is understandably a celebration of coming home. It is also true Tin Pan Alley stuff; skillfully composed and fresh as it may be, it still has a totally timeless quality. It wouldn't be a surprise if one were to hear that "New York State Of Mind" were written in the thirties or forties, when virtually all American popular music (the mainstream stuff, not cowboy songs, gospel, or Dixieland) was being written on the island of Manhattan.

Joel has a lot to say about New York; running 6:00, this is the longest track on *Turnstiles.* The opening features the kind of easy, jazzy, twirling piano riffs Billy probably played hundreds of times in his days as a lounge entertainer. As he does on so many of his songs, Billy comes in totally by himself at the outset, establishing melody and message before the rest of the orchestration makes itself felt a verse of two down the line. This is archetypally mellow music; the strings are unobtrusive, and Richie Cannata's saxophone is full-bodied but very much just a part of the scenery rather than the headliner. He does, however, carry on a direct dialogue with Joel's voice at the end, when Billy dabbles and prolongs the last couple of lines.

In "New York State Of Mind," Billy observes that while "some folks like to get away, take a holiday from the neighborhood" and head someplace warm and exotic, he's at a point in his life where he's ready for the good, solid, familiar reality of the Big Apple.

He had left the East Coast a couple of years back, and he'd done a lot and seen a lot in the interim—rubbed shoulders with the famous and chic, seen the mountains and the forests of the West. That, however, was then, and now "I know what I'm needing and I don't want to waste more time." By Greyhound bus, he's coming home to New York.

"New York State Of Mind," as performed by Joel, is a very sober song. The predominant feeling seems to be relief rather than joyful exuberance. He is weary of being detached. He surmises:

*"It was so easy living day by day
Out of touch with the rhythm and blues
But now I need a little give and take
'The New York Times, and Daily News.'"*

What he seeks is a foundation, something he can get a grip on. And that is what good old New York can offer him.

There have been plenty of love songs written to the biggest city in the U.S.A., but not too many recently. "New York State Of Mind" is definitely the best one to come out of the seventies; the fact that so many Gothamites have taken it to heart is not surprising. But its significance goes beyond such local considerations; it is a classic composition about coming home, about touching base with the things by which one can measure oneself. *That* has a meaning for folks in Paducah, Peoria, Provo, and Pawtucket as well.

On "James," the first song on side two of *Turnstiles,* the dominant instrument is an electric piano that lends an ecclesiastical tone to the proceedings. Serious business is at hand—the evaluation of the past and present of long-time chum James, a fellow for whom great expectations were maintained. For much of the song, Joel is the only instrumentalist of note. However, after he makes a few points about James, Richie Cannata comes in on soprano saxophone with passages that seem very much intended to second the motion put on the floor by Billy.

Everybody has the kind of friend Joel describes in "James"—a guy you knew in the very beginning, the kind of guy with whom you talked about what you were gonna be and how you were gonna turn out. The kind of guy you were really close with and promised you'd always remain close to; of course, by time and circumstance, it never quite stayed that way.

The fateful moment for these two came, as Billy notes, when "I went on the road—You pursued an education." To the often asked question "will you ever write your masterpiece," the answer for James would seem to be no. Sympathetically, Billy Joel seems to understand the fate of the Jameses of the world, the people who are looked to by so many people for so much that it is no longer left for them to shape their own fate or identity. "You were so relied upon," declares Billy to James, who is still "carrying the weight of the family pride."

James, possibly a prodigy of sorts, is the kind of guy who is damned by other people's projections even before he gets out of the starting gate; he's the one who gets voted "most likely to succeed" in high school, even though success will always certainly elude him. Friend Joel wants to know:

*"will you always stay
Somebody else's dream of who you are."*

In any case hope remains, he advises his chum "do what's good for you, or you're not good for anybody." The absolutely final verdict on James isn't in, but the prognosis isn't promising.

This is more than just an interesting

56

Jeffrey Mayer

character study of one particular James. The message seems to be that we should live our own lives and not allow others to dictate what's best for us. That can be an enormous and suffocating trap; it seems to have engulfed James.

It would also be interesting to speculate how much of himself Joel has put into James. In his life and career, Joel has been the recipient of floods of advice, as much of it disastrous as it is well-meaning. "James," among other things, could be a vow to stand on his own.

The bipartite "Prelude/Angry Young Man" follows. "Prelude" is the only purely instrumental piece on *Turnstiles*. It begins as a rocking affair with DeVitto scurrying all over his drum kit (the man at times seems possessed of more than two hands) and with Billy playing two totally separate lines on the piano—quick trills with the right, a deep solid drone with his left. Curiously, it smoothly metamorphoses into something western, especially with the addition of a harmonica. In fact, the end of "Prelude" almost sounds like it could be bringing us back into "The Ballad Of Billy The Kid" on *Piano Man*. Instead, we are taken for a brisk gallop into "Angry Young Man."

A gallop is exactly what it is; DeVitto sets a very fast pace here as Billy, double-tracking his own voice, spins off a series of quick couplets about the proud and stubborn "Angry Young Man."

Generally, *Turnstiles* is more sympathetic than earlier Joel albums, reflecting perhaps some feeling of inner peace. "Angry Young Man" is the one reminder here of exactly how acerbic Billy can be. Still, it is nowhere near as scathing as, say, "Captain Jack." There is something in Billy's approach that suggests this "Angry Young Man" should be pitied a little.

This politically active and inflexible young man "refuses to bend, he refuses to crawl" and is "proud of his scars and the battles he's lost"; martyrdom and persecution are obviously part of his nature as well. While "his intentions are good," this young man never accomplish anything at all. But his greatest joy seems to come from being known as what he is—an angry young man.

And how does Billy Joel feel about all this? We don't have to guess; he tells us straight out in a voice that is perhaps a bit pompous and certainly very self-assured:

I believe I've passed the age of consciousness and righteous rage,
I found that just surviving was a noble fight.
I once believed in causes too,
I had my pointless point of view,
And life went on no matter who was wrong or right.

Those sentiments are common seventies postradical fallout, but expressed far better than most folks have been able to verbalize them. The angry young man, who seems to be operating with blinders on, cannot perceive certain realities, certain changes in time and situation. Events have no impact on him; they do not change his mind. And although Billy Joel can half-heartedly salute the angry one's honor, courage, fairness, and truth, the upshot of it is that this fellow is exceedingly tedious and will "go to the grave as an angry old man."

Joel's sentiments here are certainly not ambiguous; it's time to face facts and move into the mid-seventies. There may be a place for the angry young man, but there is also room for a dinosaur—as a museum piece.

"I guess at one time or another I've been an angry young man," Billy would state later in a *Feature* interview, "but I wrote that particular song to say that there are professional angry young men, who have no principles or philosophy except to be angry."

"Angry Young Man" ends quite suddenly and segues into "I've Loved These Days," to which its relationship is like day and night. "I've Loved These Days," is sedate, contemplative, and reflective, a looking back on the recent past.

Musically, "I've Loved These Days" develops like many of Joel's songs—one piece at a time. The exposition is just Billy by himself; as we learn a little bit about "these days," lush strings are added to convey the majesty Joel describes. Then, as the singer talks about day to day movement (and the lack of it), Liberty DeVitto comes in with his bottom-heavy drums to convey a feeling of walking in place, or limbs anchored by inactivity. Finally, a distant French horn, which is replaced by a saxophone as the sound gets nearer, is every bit as sweet as the champagne Billy drinks in "I've Loved These Days." These various instruments aren't just there to make sounds; they tell the story almost as much as the words do. Producer Joel has textured an excellent bit of musical impressionism here; the "meaning" of sounds would be explored even further on *The Stranger* and *52nd Street* with producer Phil Ramone.

"I've Loved These Days" is about living high—and ultimately empty. The singer and his woman are Cole Porter or Noel Coward types updated for the seventies. They haven't a care in the world ("so nonchalant . . . so bon vivant"), their life is silk, chandeliers, champagne, cocaine, and cavier, all described in jaded detail by Billy. Such good fortune may be temporary and short-lived ("we know it's all a passing phase"), and increasing sloth, sleep, and body weight do dictate a change, but Joel can fondly state without regret, "I've loved these days."

"I've Loved These Days" has an exquisite set of lyrics; the life detailed here seems to be a dreamlike state. It is probably a mixture of fact and fantasy. Before he ended his Hollywood exile and headed home to New York, Joel may have felt engulfed by encroaching decadence. However, he hadn't yet experienced the level of success that would make the measure of opulence described herein affordable.

Pleasurable as it is, it is life on a treadmill; "we get so high and get nowhere." So it's time to get off, but Billy vows to enjoy these indulgences until the final possible moment: "we'll drink a toast to how it's been."

In a period when the word "decadence" is so frequently tossed about, and when it seems to be the life's work of myriad publicity seekers, it is surprising that more people haven't done cover versions of "I've Loved These Days." It possesses a unique kind of foggy beauty, merely a trace of sadness, and mainly a promise to begin again. It's a very accessible song.

The final track on *Turnstiles* is "Miami 2017 (Seen The Lights Go Out On Broadway)," which may be Billy Joel's only piece of recorded science-fiction. Intriguingly, he sings this number in such a matter-of-fact manner, without a trace of alarm, that it takes a few moments to glean exactly what he's telling us. The result is a colorful and vivid glimpse of life as it could be forty years or so down the line.

The first sound you hear on "Miami 2017" is the muted peal of a siren in the distance. The song builds slowly, with a trickling piano, as Billy begins to recall the apocalyptical events that befell New York. Soon, however, he's moving in full stride, with sniping guitar riffs propelling the tale along.

Joel the narrator is now comfortably situated in Florida; the events he relates are already very much a part of the past;

in fact,

*"they say a handfull still survive
To tell the world about
The way the lights went out."*

"Miami 2017" details the destruction of New York; however, it is a mystery yarn which leaves questions unanswered. For one, who are "They," the force that is orchestrating the devastation? And why are "They" doing it?

"They" are pretty arbitrary:

*"They said that Queens could stay
They blew the Bronx away
And sank Manhattan out at sea."*

While much of the city is being laid waste, New Yorkers are being pretty blasé about it. When Harlem is set on fire, no one thinks much of it, figuring the ghetto always burns. When Forty-second Street lies in ruins, hardly anyone notices, since its normal state is fairly close to that anyway. Other business proceeds as usual; boats holding refugees scheduled to depart from the Battery never sail, thanks to a strike.

The reasons behind all this remain cryptic, but that is the author's prerogative; he has still painted a fascinating scenario. The musical arrangement might have been a bit punchier and more emphatic, thus making this an even more dramatic number. But it is still quite provocative and highly original, perhaps the germ of a decent screenplay.

"Miami 2017" wraps up *Turnstiles*. Eight songs might not seem like enough, but one of the reasons you're left wanting more is because none of them have been clinkers. From the munificent "New York State Of Mind" to the frivolous "All You Wanna Do Is Dance" to the reflective "I've Loved These Days," Joel has tackled the widest scope of subjects and moods yet on any of his first three Columbia albums. He was maturing artistically and personally. If his songwriting impressed a bit more than his musical execution—well, the difference is slight. The raw materials were there to be honed by an outsider who would become a very welcome insider on the next Joel album.

Turnstiles came out in May 1976. A month later, Billy began a concert tour with a WNEW-FM live broadcast from New York's Bottom Line. The tour, consisting of 108 shows, featured three sell-out concerts at Carneigie Hall. New York was as glad to have Billy as Billy was to have New York.

Michael Putland/Retna

CHAPTER 5

Of the first track on *Turnstiles*, "Say Goodbye To Hollywood," Billy would state in a *High Fidelity* article, "It was like leaving a whole school of production with the ten million strings and the divebomber effects. I just had this thought of the Ronettes with their beehive hairdos."

Appropriately, "Say Goodbye To Hollywood" became even better known as a 1977 comeback vehicle for Ronnie Spector, former wife of production wizard Phil Spector. Ronnie, when she was still known as Veronica Bennett, had been lead singer of the Ronettes on such now classic songs as "Be My Baby" and "Walking In the Rain" in the early sixties.

Ronnie's talents are legend, and in his liner notes to her single of "Say Goodbye To Hollywood" on Epic's Cleveland International label, Dave Marsh observes, "it only takes about 15 seconds to realize that the magic is back." Her performance, notes Marsh, is "once more that invitingly ominous mix of innocence and temptation."

This rendition of "Say Goodbye To Hollywood" was arranged and produced by Miami Steve Van Zandt, who wrote the flip side, "Baby Please Don't Go." Van Zandt is a Bruce Springsteen and Southside Johnny colleague, and the connections here are deep. Springsteen is a Phil Spector fan who consciously emulated Phil's production techniques on his *Born To Run* album. Ronnie Spector made her first concert appearances in several years (outside of assorted rock & roll revivals) with Southside Johnny and the Asbury Jukes. The backup band on this single is Springsteen's E Street Band, and Bruce himself is depicted on the cover sleeve, being hugged by Ronnie.

The sound of this "Say Goodbye To Hollywood" is not surprisingly, very Springsteenish, especially since Clarence Clemons's saxophone is the featured instrument. This is a lot hotter than Joel's recording of his song. The sound here is hot, sweaty, pulsating, and urban —it's perfect music to accompany protagonist Bobby as he's "driving through the city tonight."

Indeed, such a stupendous job by Ronnie, Steve, and the E Street lads only underscores the extent to which Billy Joel was not getting the most out of his own material. His "Say Goodbye To Hollywood" is positively pallid in comparison to Ronnie's; she imbues the tune with the vitality and excitement it deserves. Listen to her do justice to this one and you realize that the author has written himself quite a song.

Ronnie's record got a lot more airplay than Billy's. And it took some time before the public came to realize that the credit for compositional magnificence should go to Billy Joel. Ronnie was so

61

closely identified with the Springsteen gang during this period that more than a few folks assumed that "Say Goodbye To Hollywood" was written by Bruce or Steve Van Zandt. Only when deejays started playing Ronnie and Billy's versions back to back did people begin to understand that the creator was the man from Hicksville.

The most recent "Say Goodbye" cover version is probably the treatment by Nigel Olsson, formerly a drummer for Elton John, on his album *Nigel.* The drum intro is a bit heavier than usual—this is a drummer's record, remember—and while Ronnie Spector was chiefly abetted by a tenor sax, the major instrumental impetus here comes from assorted electronic keyboards. Except for a backing chorus that plays around with the lyrics a little, Olsson's recording pays attention to what Billy Joel wrote. However, Nigel, who produced the track with Curt Becher, sings rather dispassionately in an unremarkable tenor. The presence of "Say Goodbye To Hollywood" on this disk might contribute somewhat to its sales, but it is not a major part of the recorded Billy Joel oeuvre.

Two of the better cover versions of other Billy Joel compositions were part of the Fantasy Records release *Midnight Prowl,* by a singer-pianist known as Angelo. The bearded Angelo, on an excellent but totally neglected album that also included a rousing rendition of John Fogerty's "Have You Ever Seen the Rain," does his own interpretations of "I've Loved These Days" and "Miami 2017 (Seen The Lights Go Out On Broadway)."

Angelo, in a gruffer and deeper voice than Billy's, masterfully captures the casual and fading elegance described in the lyrics of "I've Loved These Days." Abetted by John Blakeley's sighing guitar, Angelo projects a feeling of weary indulgence, almost relief that these days have come to an end. The lyric suggests nonchalance, but the poignancy Angelo adds to it is effective emotionally. This remake may be better than the original.

His "Miami 2017" is a good raving rocker, perhaps a bit upbeat for an apocalypse. The words are so strong, and Angelo is such a natural singer, that this track remains interesting even if music and lyric don't particularly go hand in hand here.

All things considered, Angelo does very well by the writer here, and Billy should be gratified by the tribute. To what extent the album broadened the audience for Joel's music is open to question. Considering its high quality, *Midnight Prowl* was mysteriously ignored by radio stations and the buying public.

"New York State of Mind" has been recorded and performed by countless singers, most of who profess some degree of New York chauvinism. Bette Midler's version is one of the finer ones, but the interpretation that gained the largest listening audience and did much to re-establish Joel's prowess as a songwriter before the success of *The Stranger* was by Barbra Streisand.

After hearing something like this, people were bound to ask, "who wrote that?" The answer, surprising to many who thought of him as the purveyor of little piano ditties, was Billy Joel. The widespread currency given to "New York State of Mind" by Streisand and many others may have been Billy Joel's biggest step toward respectability as a writer.

CHAPTER 6

Elizabeth

By now, Billy had married Elizabeth, with whom he had lived in California. Her contribution to the Joel success saga cannot be overrated. She has been his manager since 1976.

When they first met, Elizabeth was eighteen and pregnant and Billy was seventeen. She was married to drummer Jon Small. As Billy told *Newsday*'s Maureen Early, "I would hang out in front of their place looking very hungry. She was always a good cook and those great smells would be coming from their door. I had a lot of dinners at their place. We were great friends before we were anything else.

Billy and Elizabeth tied the knot in 1973. "If you can't trust your wife to manage you, who can you trust?" Billy told Jim Jerome about his mate and manager. "She's the family capitalist. She knows if I get my hands on bread, I'll blow it. My management doesn't know that I still have a credit card. If I can pay the bills, eat in nice restaurants twice a week and live in a nice place, that's enough. Sure it's easy for me to say now that I don't give a shit about money. But I've been poor and happy, too."

By late 1976, Billy's business affairs were so messy that he was jokingly suggesting that his wife should manage him.

It turned out to be no joke. She set to work on his garbled business situation (he'd gotten less than $8,000 in royalties from *Piano Man*) and arranged for Phil Ramone to produce *The Stranger.*

As Billy's manager, Elizabeth told Maureen Early, her job is to "decide what's necessary to be done, make sure that everybody knows what they have to do, then see that they do it."

Joel told Timothy White that Elizabeth "won't let me get into any of these crappy, ripoff situations—like a weird TV show where I come off a fool."

One of Elizabeth's achievements was a final solution to Billy's obligations to Family Productions. Artie Ripp, quoted in *Feature,* explained, "Family Productions has its logo on every Billy Joel record and gets part of the royalties every time a Billy Joel record is sold, but Billy Joel controls his life." The company logo, which resembles Romulus and Remus being nursed by a wolf, is still on Billy's Columbia albums.

While Billy's stock as a songwriter was soaring, he had not come up with a single to match the early success of "Piano Man."

"I'm not down on it," he said of the need for hit singles, in a *High Fidelity* interview shortly before his long winning-streak began. "I just can't get hung up in it. 'Piano Man' was the biggest hit, but what does that mean? That I should keep writing songs like 'Piano Man'—Son of Piano Man, Piano Man Three, Volume Four?"

There has yet to be a live Billy Joel album, but in 1977 a tape of four Joel songs recorded in concert was made available to radio stations. It helped create a great deal of additional interest in Joel and soon was being sent out to disc jockeys in album form as an item called *Souvenir.* Side one features the live cuts, and side two includes some standout tracks from the first three Columbia albums, as a renewed effort was being made to push those. The retread tracks were "Captain Jack" from *Piano Man,* "The Entertainer" and "Los Angelenos" from *Streetlife Serenade,* and "I've Loved These Days" and "Say Goodbye to Hollywood" from *Turnstiles.*

The live side was recorded before an enthusiastic audience at Palmer Auditorium at the University of Connecticut at New London, on December 5 and 6, 1976. This is Billy Joel captured on a good night.

"The Ballad of Billy The Kid" is delivered in a manner quite faithful to the original version; the vocal is nearly identical to the studio cut, but the instrumental backing is perhaps a bit more frantic and intense.

"Summer, Highland Falls" is next and shows that Joel had, by this time, become a master of pop material and a truly first-class keyboard player. The cascading piano arpeggio on this tune is no easy task; the precision and timing required are indeed demanding. But here, in mid-concert, Joel is up to the task, and his resonant tenor is also in good form.

A very long "New York State of Mind" includes a sampling of Billy's banter with the audience. This is evidence that he can be witty and personable and charming, quite contrary to the image many listeners had of him on the basis of his recordings.

Joel, in his Long Island accent, explains how he wanted to write a standard, something that Ray Charles might record, "something you'd hear on a juke box in an Italian restaurant." The bit of mimicry he then breaks into is not of Ray Charles but of any number of interchangeable Italian crooners who appear in Las Vegas.

Billy proceeds to set the scene for "New York State of Mind." It's a jazz club on the West Side of Manhattan.

David Gahr

"There's a lot of good jazz clubs on the West Side," he explains. "There's a lot of good *crime,* too. But it makes the jazz club better, because you made it through the crime." "You're feeling pretty good. You had a good couple of drinks," he continues, his audience rapt. "It's getting to be about three o'clock in the morning. You had a *good* couple of drinks. You're like one drink away from being a total asshole."

The Connecticut crowd howls in appreciation of the image. "But you're not there yet. You got one drink's grace, right? So you're still cool." This state of mind established, Joel proceeds to demonstrate, with the help of his backups, how a jazz ensemble comes on in one of these smoky little nightspots. Alternating between Cannata's organ and his own piano, with his rhythm section behind him, Joel creates a jazz intro that is exaggerated in its mellow coolness—and totally appropriate to the mood he has just described.

From here, he goes right into "New York State of Mind," which has justifiably become an anthem for those who live in and love the Apple and those who miss it from afar. His singing here is particularly impassioned. There is plenty of room for a long saxophone solo, and Joel teasingly extends the final few chords before an audience that awaits the climax like most folks hover over a slow bottle of ketchup. Altogether, a bravura performance.

The last song is the very brief and soft "Souvenir," a wistful ballad that serves the purpose of a Brahms lullaby ("Go To Sleep") or "Taps." It sends the crowd home to bed in good stead.

The *Souvenir* album was never released commercially by Columbia, but copies of it have made their way into numerous record stores. In the past couple of years, for a variety of reasons, many records have come to be classified as collector's items, and that usually means you'll have to shell out an exorbitant amount of money for them. *Souvenir* is no exception; at one midtown New York store it was selling for $20.

Billy Joel fans can decide for themselves if the price is worth it; many have apparently decided in the affirmative, because what copies did exist of *Souvenir* were selling briskly. It does include material available nowhere else, and the live cuts are excellent. And it is coupled with some of the finest selections from Joel's early albums. For true aficionados, *Souvenir* might be worth the high price.

In 1977, when the time came for a followup to *Turnstiles*, there was no doubt about who he would use as backup. He explained "love me, love my band," in reference to Stegmeyer, Cannata, and DeVitto. "These guys go out on the road nine months a year. They know the material better than anybody."

Doug Stegmeyer is a long-time Joel cohort, and his bass was first heard on the *Turnstiles* album. "He's really steady, kind of locked to my left hand," Billy says of Doug. "I mean he doesn't play like Stanley Clarke or Jaco Pastorius—he's from the Paul McCartney less-is-more school of bass playing—which is almost harder to play than the other way. And he put this band together." Doug had played in a Long Island aggregation called Topper with Liberty DeVitto, and he introduced Billy to Liberty in time for the drummer to also make the *Turnstiles* sessions.

Of Liberty, who formerly played behind Detroit rock legend Mitch Ryder, Billy states, "he is a real Italian rock 'n' roller, from y'know, *crazy*. He's got tons of energy, the group comedian, the guy who wrecks things on the road."

Ken Regan/Camera 5

Jeffrey Mayer

Another ex-Topper member, guitarist Russell Javors, played on much of *Turnstiles* and is part of the Billy Joel concert band. However, the guitar lines on most of *The Stranger* and *52nd Street* have largely been the work of Steve Khan, usually referred to as Mr. Steve Kahn, who is, as they say, a star in his own right.

Kahn, a leading exponent of what is usually termed fusion music, is one of the most respected guitarists in America. Khan has several solo albums to his credit and is also prominently featured on *Montreux Summit* and the best-selling *Alivemutherforya* with Billy Cobham, Tom Scott, Alphonso Johnson, and Mark Soskin. Khan's distinctive style has added an important new voice and counterpoint to Billy Joel's repertoire.

The other Joel regular is Richie Cannata, also from Long Island, whose premier instrument is the tenor sax but who also plays clarinet and organ. Cannata's appearances on *The Stranger* and *52nd Street* have lent a gutsy new element to Joel's tunes and have given the songs the kind of urban influence the author seems to be seeking. On record, at least, Richie is to Billy pretty much what Clarence Clemons is to Bruce Springsteen.

As for himself, Joel explains that he tries to do his vocals live in the studio. "There's something between my voice and the piano. I don't think I sing as well when I'm not playing."

In an interview that was to appear just after the next album, *The Stranger,* was released, Joel had some thoughts on the manner in which the press had virtually ignored him.

"Just after 'Piano Man' came out, I was like the darling of the press," he told *High Fidelity* writer Susan Elliot. "You know, they like to pick up on unknowns and make them their little heroes. I was new to the success thing, so I figured, 'Oh wow! I'm King Kong—I'm great!" That was 1973. Now it's four years later and I'm an old dog and I can't get hung up in that anymore. If a record's a hit, that's nice. I just write songs."

At the time, Joel didn't know that *The Stranger,* his first album with producer Phil Ramone, would be much more than a mere "hit."

CHAPTER 7

"The Stranger"

Joel and Ramone recorded *The Stranger* at A&R Recording in New York. Stegmeyer and DeVitto again constituted the rhythm section, with Cannata on woodwinds and organ. Steve Khan and Hiram Bullock were the chief guitarists, although Steve Burgh and Hugh McCracken appeared on several tracks. The orchestrations were done by Patrick Williams. All but one of the songs are 1977 compositions—the exception is "Everybody Has A Dream," which was written back in 1971 but put off for recording until this session six years later.

The black and white photography for *The Stranger* by Jim Houghton is the most striking yet on a Billy Joel album. On the cover, a barefoot Billy sits on an unmade bed (is it worth remembering that Paul McCartney was barefoot on "Abbey Road"?). He stares, attentively but casually, at the pillow beside him. On it rests the mask of a woman's face; merely a mask, no body at all. Billy's expression does not suggest that this is unusual.

The back cover is far less mysterious. It's Billy in his natural milieu, in the kind of situation that could give birth to

David Gahr

much of the material on *The Stranger.* Here are Billy and a bunch of his regular pals relaxing in a friendly neighborhood restaurant, probably Italian. And the regular pals are Stegmeyer, DeVitto, Cannata, and Phil Ramone. Here's Billy at home, where folks can drink and dress casually (Ramone in a Yankee-uniform shirt). Only Billy is in a suit, but it's a decidedly working class one—white coat, dark shirt, and garish tie.

"New York has a kind of jazz influence on me," he has said, "and I've been leaning more into jazzier things to give Richie (Cannata) a chance to blow." As far as jazziness is concerned, *The Stranger* also has important contributions by Khan, the fusion guitarist, and by alto-sax player Phil Woods.

Side one kicks off with "Movin' Out (Anthony's Song)," originally projected as the first single from *The Stranger.* The decision to issue it first would seem to have been an unusual one; it is a very good track, but it isn't your typical Top-40 AM-radio fare by any means. Its message is quite pointed, and its story is told in rich detail. Top-40 hits are usually simple and so accessible that you can grasp their essence whilst dodging traffic on the way to work. And they are rarely as polemical as "Movin' Out"; an artist has got to have an AM audience warm to him before he can hit them with something like this. After they love him they'll be ready to embrace more of his portfolio.

"Movin' Out" is about the hard-working and the restless. In staccato, attacking fashion, Joel tells us of a couple of people who bust their backs at dead-end jobs in the hope that it will get them the fulfillment of their dream somewhere down the line. But Joel's point here is that the dream doesn't justify such a paltry existence; either the goal isn't worth it, or it ain't worth it if you've got to destroy yourself getting there.

There's Anthony himself, who sweats in the grocery store "savin' his pennies for someday." It's a moot point which will come first—his heart attack or his house in Hackensack. "Is that what you

United Press International

get with your money?" is Joel's logical reaction. Such a value system is not for him:

*"If that's what it's all about
If that's movin' up then I'm movin' out."*

The other protagonist, Sergeant O'Leary, is also a living burlesque of the work ethic. By day he treads his police beat; by night he stands and serves behind the bar at Mister Cacciatore's (terrific name). He sees his destiny as a Cadillac owner, a step up from his trusty Chevy, but he may be in no condition to enjoy the day when it comes:

*"if he can't drive with a broken back
At least he can polish the fenders."*

At the end, after Joel reaffirms his distaste for such a lifestyle and opts for "Movin' out," he does just that. There is the sound of a car pulling up, the door slamming, and the same car rushing off into the distance; it is literal distance that he is putting between himself and the dreary lives he has depicted. His point well taken is hereby dramatically underscored.

"Movin' Out" is not one of the more musically complex songs on the album, but it is the first indication that great care has gone into choosing the best and most appropriate sounds to accompany these compositions. The instruments used are mainly bottom heavy, just right for such morose subject matter. More importantly, every time Joel makes a major point, there is an instrument there to underline it. It may be Cannata's saxophone, which is uplifting when Joel pleads for a more uplifting existence, or it may be Liberty's solid bass drum, which he slams with his feet the moment Joel slams the car door. The music is making its point in tandem with the lyric; that kind of pairing makes for a very effective album.

The title song "The Stranger" is up next. It is cushioned by soft, lovely, four-o'clock-in-the-morning dabbling at the piano, with some of the melody accompanied by high predawn whistling. These lilting strains leave us a bit unprepared for the sudden drama of the actual tune, a piece of funk sung by Joel in cautious and confidential "this is between you and me" tones.

Among other things, this song answers the mystery behind the strange disembodied mask on the album's front cover. "The Stranger" is all about masks and faces and people who hide behind false ones. The real face is often known only to oneself; and the whole truth and nothing but the truth is not even entrusted to our most cherished companions:

*"though we share so many secrets
There are some we never tell."*

Keeping this in mind, Joel further suggests that we should never be surprised by "the stranger" in the people we thought we knew best; did we ever let them see *our* innermost secrets?

The construction of "The Stranger" is uncanny. The quiet opening more or less cleanses our minds and puts us at rest. Then, quite briskly, a very strong object lesson is shoved in our ears and faces. Finally, the soft section returns at the end, giving us a chance to let Joel's message sink in. There is a respite for pause and reflection. Few musicians and producers will tell you something, tell you to think about it, and then actually give you a *chance* to think about. It is a nice technique; it should be used more often.

One interesting musical note about "The Stranger" regards Billy's singing in the choruses. On the verses he uses his "natural" voice; on the choruses, he is doubletracked and sings in much loftier registers. You'd be tempted to call it falsetto because it's so high, but it's not falsetto; the guy can get up that high without straining or contriving his vocal cords. We're seeing the next step in Joel's growth as a crooner. He is expanding his range, and he can control it.

"The Stranger" is followed by "Just The Way You Are." By now this is Billy's best-known song, and it is perhaps *the* love song of the late seventies. It's the kind of tune couples can actually be heard singing to each other; apparently Joel managed to touch a feeling that dwelt in the hearts of a lot of people—millions of them.

In the course of "Just The Way You Are," Joel reassures his lover (the song is for wife Elizabeth) of his faithfulness and good intentions on almost every imaginable level, from the opening line "Don't go changing, to try and please me" and beyond. He will not take her for granted, he will not desert her when things are bad, he will not ask her to be someone she is not. She doesn't have to worry about being fashionable; he just wants her to be "the same old someone that I knew."

By the final verse, Billy is saying everything that the throngs of people who made the single and the album a smash must love to hear:

*"I said I love you and that's forever
And this I promise from the heart
I could not love you any better
I love you just the way you are."*

These feelings are solemnized in a masterfully textured framework. We hear the sweet sounds of Billy's electric piano; the solid and consistent background drone (of what instrument or voice?) that sounds like angels humming; the acoustic guitars of Hugh McCracken and Steve Burgh (Steve Forbert's producer), which lend an earthbound body to Billy's heavenly sentiments; and the alto-saxophone solos by guest performer Phil Woods, whom many critics consider the best current practitioner of that particular woodwind. In the first couple of solos, Woods seems to paint light and airy colors around Billy's big picture. But his last passages show why the sax is considered such a sensuous instrument—it speaks love; it says "romance."

Those who badmouthed "Just The Way You Are" (the numbers were noticeable only after stations began playing it fifty times or more a day) considered it syrupy and oversentimentalized; others thought it was a bit patronizing, since Billy seemed to be dictating to this unseen woman, albeit beneficently.

Joel, however, hadn't intended anything other than romantic stuff; and his sentiments seem sincere, particularly considering the close true-life relationship on which the song is based. As for being patronizing—well, we hear only one half of the dialogue, and the structure of the story suggests that these are the things she needs to hear and he needs to say. The two of them seem to have a mutual give-and-take; and this song can be covered by female singers as well as males.

A Billy Joel mural, "Scenes From An Italian Restaurant," starts with the star playing the melody line on a piano; then, just to make sure we know this is an *Italian* restaurant, we hear an accordion played by Dominic Cortese.

There is a kaleidoscope of scenes and sounds on this selection that runs 7:35. It is like a miniature symphony with several movements. The first part is purely exposition—the invitation to celebrate over a bottle of wine at the corner spot where the singer and his cronies have apparently hoisted many a glass in the past.

Joel has commented that he con-

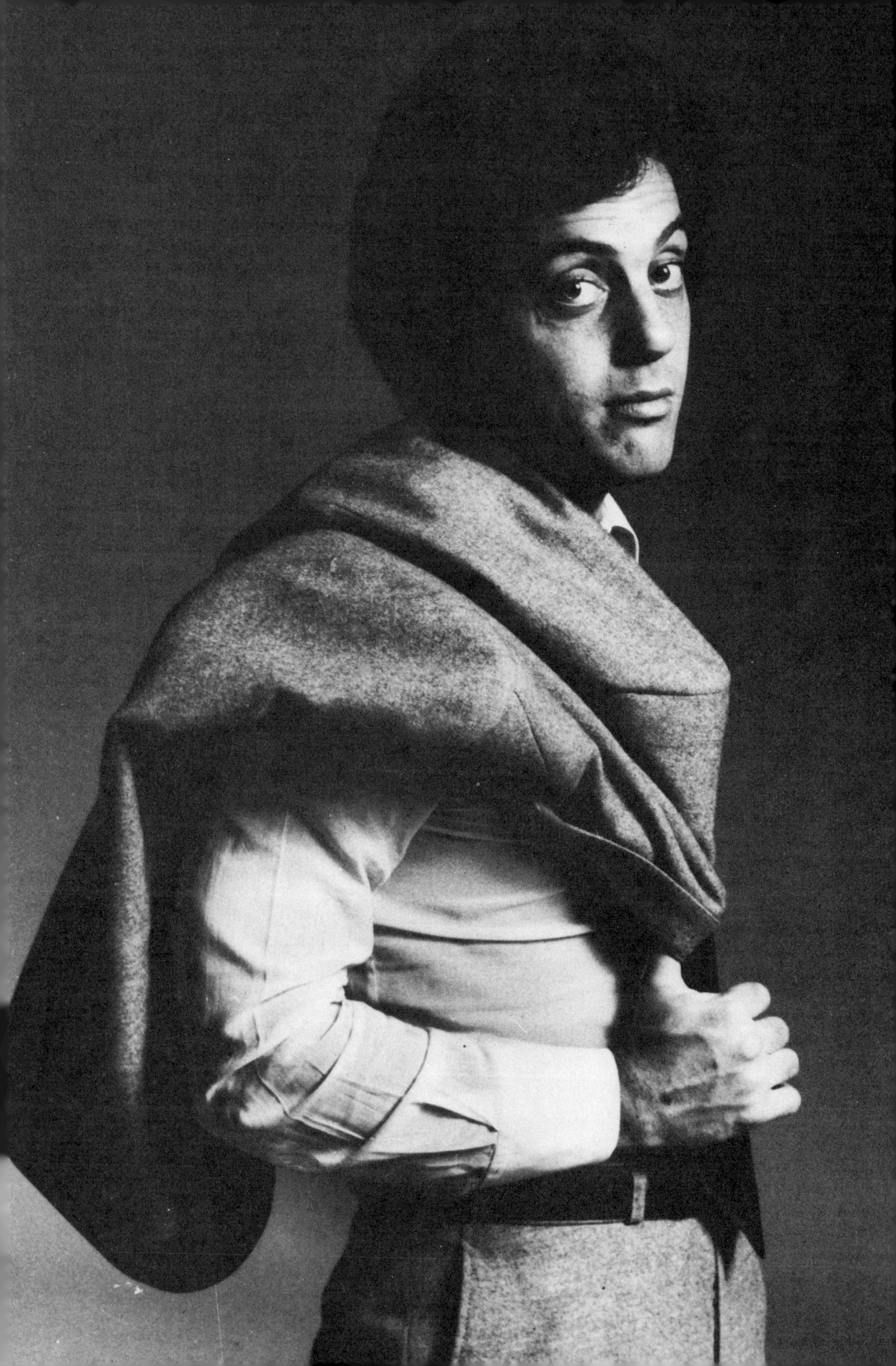

sciously went for a more urban sound on *The Stranger*. That city feel is there and much of it is because of the saxophone stylings of Richie Cannata. After the initial setting of the scene in the Italian restaurant, Cannata steps forward with a transition that is rich, fluid, and evocative; it is an emotional crescendo. It is so scintillating that its impact is that of a magic carpet, and in fact it does transport us back into the author's memories of some of the personalities he has known at the restaurant and other haunts.

Those memories are triggered by a meeting with one of those old friends. Much time has passed since their last meeting; in fact, the singer's entire life has changed:

*"Got a good job, got a good office
Got a new wife, got a new life."*

It's a far cry from the days when these two were buddies, "hanging out at the village green" in "engineer boots, leather jackets and tight blue jeans." Those were the singer's "sweet romantic teenage nights" and as he recalls them, Cannata emerges again; he has switched from tenor to soprano sax and his phrasing here is sprightly, chipper, and carefree, very appropriate for a time when one's only responsibility was to enjoy oneself.

The next movement of this symphony is launched on the wings of Billy's suddenly swift and rocking piano and Liberty DeVitto's solid and steady drumming. This section, the longest part of "Scenes," is a rocker all the way, with Cannata on tenor again, in the manner of the great red-faced saxmen of the Bill Haley era, and Joel darting from one end of the keyboard to the other, more nimbly than anyone this side of Jerry Lee Lewis.

This section focuses on the activities of Brenda and Eddie, clearly the golden couple of the singer's adolescent days. It might seem strange that a meeting with an old chum would trigger a reminiscence of two other people. However, a winning romantic couple in the suburban days of teen-ager Joel was a rare entity that could assume heroic proportions. Besides, the rise and fall of this twosome is skillfully made to epitomize the necessary and perhaps lamentable transition from frivolous and idyllic youth to the very real burdens of adulthood.

We get the entire Brenda and Eddie saga, the lifetime of a couple that in chronological terms lasted about two years. They got married despite friends' reservations about Eddie's ability as a provider. They moved in together amid typical newlywed trappings:

*"deep pile carpet
and a couple of paintings from Sears."*

as Joel cleverly informs us.

Things soon go sour for this winning twosome; true to prophecy, their dollars disappear, fights ensue, "they got a divorce as a matter of course"—an amicable one—and tried to go back to the familiar place where they'd reigned as "the king and the queen."

Alas, this is a classic "you can't go home again" situation; all that remained was for them to "pick up the pieces. We always knew they would both find a way to get by," Joel observes, but as he tells his friend, he doesn't know how they are getting by.

There's just a minute trace of ambiguity here; are they picking up the pieces of their own lives separately or together? Have they decided to give it another go or not? It would seem that the first split is final, but it's not clear here. The singer-narrator isn't aware of the latest details anyway; our guess is as good as his.

We are swept back to the present by

a magnificent string interlude orchestrated by Patrick Williams; it is truly symphonic in scope and nature; and Billy is repeating his original invitation to this rediscovered pal. He will meet him over a bottle of wine of his choice at the Italian restaurant. The invite is in the form of a denouement; and the code is once again Cannata's lush tenor sax. The man's playing is truly a thing of beauty; his performance here is the most outstanding of any of Joel's accompanists on *The Stranger,* and these are Cannata's finest moments yet on a Joel album. As far as sterling use of sax in popular music is concerned, only Bruce Springsteen's sidekick Clarence Clemons and Gerry Rafferty's "Baker Street" herald Raphael Ravenscroft were in the same league as Cannata in 1977-78.

"Scenes From An Italian Restaurant" is an ambitious construction that works, a thoroughly engrossing time trip. Brenda and Eddie themselves are not very important, but they give the author an opportunity to reflect on various stages of his life, to examine his present by revisiting his past.

"Scenes" is also a careful and considerate juxtaposition of different musical idioms that work together. This is risk taking that pays off; and it is certainly proof that Joel is not just plowing the same old turf.

Stereo Review critic Peter Reilly would refer to "Scenes From an Italian Restaurant" as "a greaser *Tristan und Isolde.*"

Side two of *The Stranger* begins with "Vienna." The mood and the music are different, but the message is essentially the same as was delivered in "Movin' Out." Joel's advice here is "slow down," and the music here *is* slowed down. His singing here is the most relaxed on the album. He is like a seasoned veteran who has done plenty and is now justified in just leaning back and admonishing the young up-and-comer, "You're so ambitious for a juvenile." Meanwhile, the mellow mood of "Vienna" is largely due to the bass and drums of Stegmeyer and DeVitto, who keep a constant pace that is just this side of standing still.

Joel tells the eager beaver that he'll get a lot of what he wants in this world but he won't ever get it all, and he'll kill himself trying if he doesn't "cool it off before you burn out." The facts of life include,

"You can't be everything you want to be Before your time."

The go-getter would do well to remove himself from circulation for a while and become incommunicado, says Joel. His success drive won't suffer irreparable damage: "you can afford to lose a day or two." The youngster's motivation? "Vienna waits for you."

Vienna is made to represent all that is escape and exotic—everything that can transport someone as far from his daily grind as possible. The street scenes of Austria are easily visualized as we hear the strains of Dominic Cortese's accordion. Anyone who thinks the accordion is just a comical instrument should pay attention here; Cortese's musicianship is very European and very beautiful. Along with Joel's easy vocalization and the steady rhythm section, it makes "Vienna" a tranquilizing trip.

"Only The Good Die Young" is not a song that grows on you—it doesn't have to. It reaches out and grabs you and makes its impact felt the first time out. The brief beginning has Billy playing a minor variation of the melody, but soon the array of acoustic guitar, handicaps, and syncopated drumming creates a "let's get a move on" urgency. There's no time to waste, and that is actually the message of Billy Joel's opening lines:

*"Come out Virginia, Don't let me wait
You Catholic girls start much too late
But sooner or later it comes down to fate
I might as well be the one."*

His intentions are obvious, and they are not honorable. One writer suggested that "Only The Good Die Young" was an ode to a girl who had spurned Billy back in his Long Island days. That may or may not be the case, but what is certain is that "Only The Good Die Young" has been Billy Joel's most controversial composition to date.

It is the only one of his songs that has been banned by radio stations. More than a few programmers prohibited it from airplay because of its supposedly volatile statements about Catholics and their morality. Billy may not have been "banned in Boston" but his song was prohibited in St. Louis.

The most highly publicized episode involving "Only The Good Die Young" occurred at Seton Hall University, an educational institution in South Orange, New Jersey. The trustees of Seton Hall's radio station banned "Only The Good Die Young," but apparently due not as much to the content of the song as to the deejays' comments about it. College students would play the lines about the sexual inhibitions of Catholic girls and then comment on the air that "it's true" and make suggestions that it would be better if it were *not* true.

The relationship between the singer and Virginia is straight out of those fifties and early sixties movies about leather-clad street toughs and the rare and unusual "good girls" who didn't join in their treacherous fun. The bad boy stands in the street and taunts the good girl, who's either standing in the doorway or meekly peeking out of her window.

The hullabaloo about "Only The Good Die Young" isn't surprising. In what is presented as a clear choice between the sacred and secular approach to life, Billy Joel comes out very strongly on the side of the secular. That kind of thing can be disturbing to folks who are sensitive about morality, religion, and related matters. There is nothing ambiguous in Billy's intent; he's not tentative or apologetic about his decision. He wants Virginia to come *out*. This instant!

Of course, there are probably more lapsed Catholics than practicing ones listening to Billy Joel records, so plenty of folks were really ready for Billy's broadside attack on Catholic sexual mores. They'd cheer him on at every turn; like him, they'd "rather laugh with the sinners than cry with the saints" because "sinners are much more fun."

"Only The Good Die Young" is a lickety-split rocker that would have appealed to a large audience even if they never bothered to listen to the words. But one of the most effective things about the performance of the song here is that the obvious joy Billy and his band are experiencing playing this music is the same kind of exuberant devil-may-care fun his hellion character is having in the lyric. "You might have heard I run with a dangerous crowd," he sings; "we ain't too pretty / we ain't too proud." Maybe so, but they make an extremely good case for their chosen ways.

In *Feature,* Billy claimed that "Only The Good Die Young" wasn't so much antireligion as prolust. "Come out Virginia! I'll tell you anything you want to hear!"

"She's Always A Woman" brings back acoustic guitarists McCracken and Burgh, who did such a lovely job on "Just The Way You Are." They play as if they are serenading an angel, which is pretty intriguing given that the first two lines talk of a woman who can "kill with a smile" and "wound with her eyes." This notion of female lethalness would be explored in greater depth on Joel's subsequent *52nd Street* album.

What Joel is presenting us with in "She's Always A Woman" is a lady for whom the words "infinitely variable" rate as an understatement. This woman can be whatever she pleases and can be it very well; she can

*"promise you more
Than the Garden of Eden
Then she'll carelessly cut you
And laugh while you're bleedin'."*

Sounds like a real sweetheart; but to Billy, she can seemingly do no wrong. She is and will always be what the title indicates.

"She's Always A Woman" may rank as the ultimate tribute to the alleged unpredictability of the female of the species and should have special appeal to anyone who believes in or likes that kind of thing. Billy apparently does; his singing on this track is rather reverential. His coruscating piano riffs wind over, around, and through the melody. This is certainly a lovely ballad; but taste in the opposite sex remains relative.

"Get It Right The First Time," with Cannata switching to flute, Ralph MacDonald supplying additional percussion, DeVitto playing a strange variation of march rhythms on the drums, Stegmeyer adding a bass line that at times approaches disco, and Steve Khan appearing intermittently with a repeated four-note guitar riff, is a bizarre fusion of many elements that aren't that appealing separately, let alone in this jumble.

This one isn't one of Joel's better tunes; it isn't terrible, but it is the least impressive track in an outstanding set. The song is basically concerned with those once-in-a-lifetime opportunities with women where you've got to make a move because there ain't no tomorrow. Even if you're not sure your favorable first impression is gonna hold up. Even if you aren't the kind of smoothie who can pull off this kind of miracle on the spot. The predicament is a real one that hordes of healthy humans can empathize with. Still, it hasn't been made into something your ears are hankering to hear.

The piano intro to "Everybody Has A Dream is evocative both of the closing theme of NBC's "Saturday Night" and Nicky Hopkins's "Girl From Mill Valley" piano solo with the Jeff Beck Group, way back in 1969 (you can look it up!).

The song's inclusion is a bit of a surprise. It is the one conscious attempt at "soulfulness," with a Booker T-style organ undercurrent, played here by Richard Tee, and an all-star soulful female backup choir which includes Phoebe Snow (another Phil Ramone client) and Patti Austin.

"Everybody Has A Dream" was also written by Joel back in 1971, making it the only song here that was not composed specifically for inclusion on *The Stranger*. As a matter of fact, its origin predates Joel's entire Columbia recording career.

Perhaps because it is the one song on *The Stranger* which seems least to epitomize Joel's current status, it is the one song on the album that did not earn considerable radio airplay. In fact, it was hardly played at all; it might be the only track here that many latter-day Billy Joel fans wouldn't recognize.

Why he waited so long to put it on here is something we are not privy to, but it is fortunate that he finally did put it on one of his records. Thematically, it is not ground-breaking; songs about having big dreams are plentiful.

It is Billy's vocalizing here that is such a revelation. At times he is beautifully soulful in Ray Charles fashion. At other times he is soft but so earnest in what is little more than a whisper. He is demonstrating a high level of emotional intensity while maintaining an extremely low level of decibels. It is not something he has attempted all that often, but here he carries it off masterfully. At moments, the effect is quite moving.

As "Everybody Has A Dream" ends, we assume the album has come to a close. But after a pause, the piano and whistling we heard at the very beginning of side one comes back. Its return was totally unexpected, but it's welcome, for it lends a kind of symmetry to *The Stranger*; it functions as bookends for all the stories told in between.

More importantly, it adds a central concept to *The Stranger* We imagine it in cinematic terms; this "stranger" is one of those guys who walks the rain-soaked streets early in the morning, with a crumpled hat pushed far back on his head, a raincoat over his shoulder, and a tie that is no longer tied. He leans against a lamppost, alone with his thoughts. And those thoughts are these nine variegated but vivid songs. Having comtemplated enough, the lone stranger walks away (his back would be to the camera), whistling as he saunters on.

The fact that *The Stranger* conjures up these and so many other visual images is one measure of the success of Joel, Ramone, and the rest of the crew. More than on any other Billy Joel album, *The Stranger* is full of people, places, and situations that truly come alive. Joel and Ramone have wedded word to sound with maximum effectiveness. *The Stranger* is an album that yields something more with each repeated listening. And *that* is the kind of record people go out and buy. And by last count, over four million folks had purchased *The Stranger*.

Stereo Review's Peter Reilly, one of the more literate rock commentators, observed wryly that *The Stranger* title "may echo the Albert Camus novel, but once into it you soon discover that it is

Michael Putland/Retna

much more like a 'Remembrance of Things Pasta,' an Italian-American nostalgia trip." He noted, however, that Joel's songs possessed "a directness that Proust would probably have found appalling."

Reilly was impressed that Joel was no dilettante, suggesting that *The Stranger* succeeded "because Joel knows his territory firsthand." He explained, "you know that the testimony you are about to hear is the truth, the whole truth, and nothing but." He concluded, "*The Stranger* isn't a particularly showy or innovative album, but it is bone-honest, filled with a very privileged kind of insight, and as gritty as life."

Susan Elliot suggested that *The Stranger* "exhibited more musical growth in one year than most writers can consummate in a decade."

In *Rolling Stone*, Billy Altman said "Movin' Out" and "Just The Way You Are" were "forced and overly simplistic," but conceded, "the imagery and melodies of *The Stranger* more often than not work." Much of the album, he said, had "a fluid sound occasionally sparked by a light soul touch."

Altman noted of Joel, "we don't expect subtlety or understatement from him and, indeed, his lyrics can be as smartassed as ever." However, the reviewer cited "She's Always A Woman" as an exception to this case.

Rolling Stone did not make *The Stranger* the lead review in its 1977 end-of-the-year issue. In fact, relatively little space was devoted to it. It may be that the magazine did not consider *The Stranger* a truly major release, because in the review Billy Joel is still more or less discussed in the future tense. Praising Phil Ramone's emphasis on sound rather than mere lyric, Altman concludes that such an approach "definitely lessens the im-

Backstage party for Billy with Phil Ramone (left), producer of The Stranger, and Walter Yetnikoff, president of CBS Records Group.

Bobby Bank

pact of the sarcasm, which in the long run may help boost Joel's career immeasurably."

After *The Stranger* came out, *Time* profiled Billy, and writer Jay Cocks observed, "Joel's best songs have the brash humor, the sad, sometimes lavish sentiment that still stirs faint echoes of the boys down on the corner, harmonizing on the Top 40." Cocks added, "There is great sympathy in these songs, observations that can be caustic and still stay fond."

Citing "Just The Way You Are" in particular, Cocks stated, "Joel harks back to the luxuriant strains of superb song craftsmen like Harold Arlen as much as he follows in the tradition of masters of rock 'n' roll delirium like Phil Spector. His songs have been covered by belters like Streisand and jazz stylists like Bobby Scott, and seem easily to snuggle into whatever groove comes up."

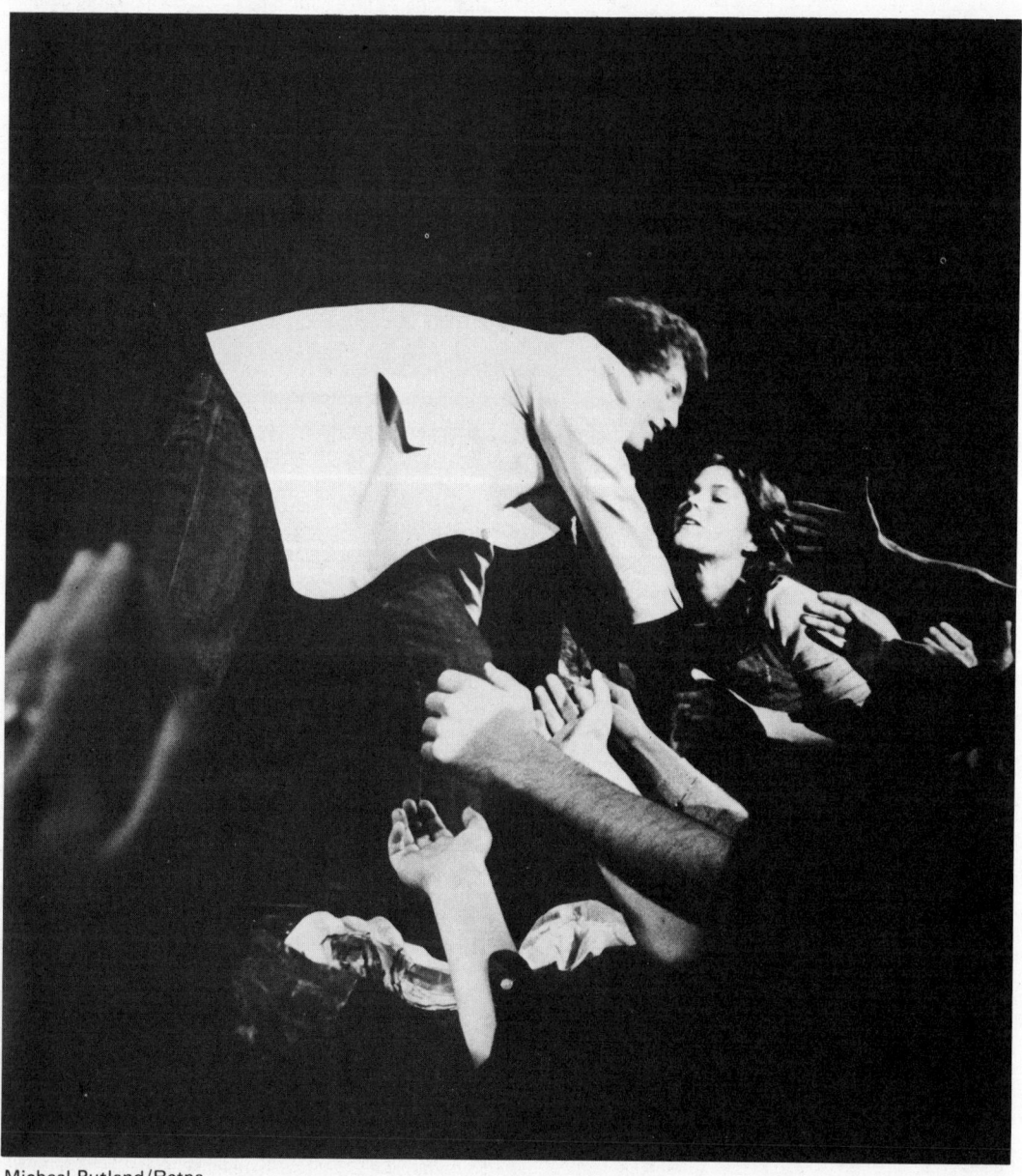

Michael Putland/Retna

CHAPTER 8

Public Acclaim

"Just The Way You Are" seemed to capture the imagination of many hearts starved for such an expression of romance. As couples strode down the aisle in 1978 and 1979, a good number of them were selecting "Just The Way You Are" as their official wedding song.

Far and away, it was the public's reception of "Just The Way You Are" that gave Joel his current hefty dose of fame. At the time, it made him wary. "I don't trust success from a single hit," he confessed. And as Jim Jerome observed, "Just The Way You Are" was not really representative of the nature and breadth of Joel's repertoire. "People who think it's me are misled," Joel told him. "Live, we do harder rock 'n' roll."

In a talk with Susan Elliot, Billy praised his new producer, Phil Ramone, highly. "He's as crazy as I am. He doesn't come off like 'I'm the producer, and we're going to do it *my* way'. He's willing to let anything happen in that studio. All these great musicians love Phil...."

He continued, "I never knew any album could be fun to make. Before it was always very clinical . . . playing to this glass booth. Only thing is, I like to be . . . spontaneous."

Perhaps Ramone's biggest plus, in Billy's eyes, was his appreciation of the guys who had been playing with Billy on the road. That appreciation was reciprocated by the band. "They'd been through

David Gahr

different producers turning them down," Billy explained. "They thought they were under the gun. When they found out the guy liked them, they grew, flowered; they blossomed."

In *Rolling Stone*, critic Stephen Holden suggested, "Billy Joel would probably still be only a cult figure, idolized in concert but poorly represented on record, if he hadn't found the perfect studio collaborator in producer Phil Ramone."

Praise for Joel as couchside companion came from an unexpected place, *Apartment Life*, a magazine that tutors young and trendy adults on how to survive and thrive in the big city. In the magazine's "1978 Instant Replay Awards," writer Barbara Rowes designated *The Stranger* the "Best Self-Help Album of the Year."

She explained "A touch of reassurance and soothing support therapy characterize the psychology of Billy Joel, who outshrinked Wayne Dyer as the voice of mental health in 1978. Like a *summa cum laude* graduate of *est*, Joel gives the best free advice in the neighborhood; It's a touching comfort that there's still someone out there who loves you 'just the way you are', and his coy philosophy unearths 'the faces of the strangers in our soul.' "

Rowes lauded Joel as "a sensitive observer of the erroneous zones of human behavior. His lyric keyboard bridges reveal delicate craftsmanship. He's the most sympathetic soul in rock today."

By late 1977, Billy Joel had definitely made good. If he hadn't been the boy most likely to suceed, he had become the one who succeeded the most. As the Hicksville Class of '67 assembled for its tenth-anniversary class reunion one spring night in Long Island, William Martin Joel could not be in attendance. He had a previous engagement, a better date. Billy Joel was making his first appearance on NBC's "Saturday Night," the most coveted video venue for popular musicians. Like Jimmy Cagney, to whom he is not so dissimilar in image and physical presence, Billy could justifiably declare, "Hey, Ma, I'm on top of the world!"

One of the little-known asides in the story of Billy's monumental success with *The Stranger* is the fact that one of the first attempts to market the album's tunes was a dismal failure.

"Movin' Out (Anthony's Song)" was the first single released from the album, and it was a little less than boffo at the box office. But almost before anyone could notice (about six weeks later, actually), Columbia responded quickly and made "Just The Way You Are" the next single. On the strength of that song, *The Stranger* quickly became a gold LP. "Just The Way You Are" was on the American singles charts for four months —and seemingly on your local Top-40 radio station every fifteen minutes.

With the public ear now attuned to the sound of the piano man, Columbia reissued "Movin' Out," and this time America was much more receptive to the preoccupations of the celebrated Anthony. It quickly moved into the Top-Twenty. "Only The Good Die Young" and "She's Always A Woman" made a grand total of four hit singles from one LP.

Trendy *People*, featuring Billy after "Just The Way You Are" became a smash, made much of his purported pugnaciousness. The article headed "If Billy Joel doesn't love you 'Just The Way You Are' don't argue" suggested Joel was "dishing out knuckle sandwiches long before Stallone."

Joel characterized himself as a "hood" and *People* characterized suburban Hicksville as "tough." The young Joel, in addition to playing hooky frequently, apparently lacked school spirit;

he didn't buy his high school class ring or yearbook.

In an interview with Jim Jerome, Joel claimed "I'm still just another heavy hitter off the street." If so, he's a slugger with a sweet side. As Jerome notes, "Just The Way You Are" was gentle enough to serve as the soundtrack during the (needlessly) controversial loss-of-virginity scene on a short-lived NBC television series called "James at 15."

Billy Joel was making news in unlikely places.

Forbes Magazine's 1978 cover article on 'Stayin' Alive in the Record Business" detailed the working relationship between Billy and Elizabeth, in a section called "They Were Maulin' Her Man."

Elizabeth has assembled seven Billy Joel companies under the umbrella Home Run Systems. According to *Forbes*, the companies stood to gross $10 million in 1978, with $4 million coming from *The Stranger* and the rest from management, music publishing, video, and magazine publishing.

Although *Piano Man*, the 1973 album, went gold in 1974, Elizabeth said it earned Billy just $7,763. "From the day he signed," she explained, "CBS was on one end, Billy on the other, and the previous production commitment was in the middle. The person in the middle seemed to be taking all the money and making the decisions."

Elizabeth's initial attraction to Billy had nothing to do with any anticipated windfall. "When we started to live together, I wasn't even sure if Billy was talented," she recalled. "I thought I might have to support him. I was in love."

In time, Elizabeth took over the bookkeeping and fired his management. "They called with a tour for Billy with a booking at the Nassau Coliseum where he opened for the Beach Boys. They consented to pay him $2,000. I told the guy on the phone, 'Go to hell, you're fired.' "

Richard E. Aaron / Thunder Thumbs

A new contract with CBS gave Billy over one dollar per record for *The Stranger.* In September 1978, Billy started a tour arranged by Elizabeth that was expected to gross $3 million and expose him to one million fans.

The Joel family wealth, clearly, is just reward for both parties. "This is a business," Elizabeth stated in the *Forbes* piece. "People never expected me to be as smart as I was, and they would be totally frank because they didn't realize I was building my empire. They taught me that money is the bottom line of everything. It's an actual, factual scale of how to see things."

In style and appearance, Billy Joel may have broken the mold for rock superstars. "Nobody ever mistook Billy Joel for a matinee idol," observed Dave Marsh. "In a world that worships angular, tall, rangy types like Robert De Niro and John Travolta, Joel is out of place. Short and thick-bodied, with eyes as enormous (and frequently as bloodshot) as Robert Mitchum's, with a busted nose and lopsided grin, Joel is a perfect Hell's Kitchen wise guy, a real-life deadend kid." *Penthouse* writer William Kowinski saw Joel as "the Cagney of the Coliseums, the Serpico of Pop."

Billy's somewhat tough image is not totally a facade. His broken nose was well-earned in a boyhood boxing match.

In contrast to Joel's cocksure image, *Feature* writer Timothy White found him to be "rather shy, ruddy-faced and muscular in a squatty way, his intense parlance often punctuated with a 'dese' or 'dose.'"

What mattered most, of course, was the quality of his product. "I think I'm good at what I do," he informed Elliot, "and if you like what you're doing that's a big part of it. So what more could I want? To be a musician and to be making a living is a miracle to begin with."

After the release of *The Stranger,* Billy played fifty-four American concerts between September 28 and December 13 of 1977 with SRO tours of Europe and Japan following those dates. The intensive gigging is probably one of the reasons *The Stranger* vaulted into the *Billboard* Top-Ten in January 1978.

By now, audiences have discovered that Joel is quite a character—several characters, in fact. Dave Marsh suggests that role playing "is at the core of his nature. Put him in an elevator with a group of well-dressed, uptight strangers and he'll start jabbering in Andy Kauffman-style gibberish, replete with gestures and grimaces that make ignoring him impossible. The band's life on the road is an endless series of one-liners, routines and put-ons" which Marsh says is "here raised nearly to an art."

Billy, whose stage apparel is a unique hodgepodge, often satirizes the wardrobes of other rock stars, and their various indulgences, in his stage monologues. He has imitated Bruce Springsteen, Bob Dylan, Paul Simon, and Randy Newman, to name a few. Recently he gave an audience his version of Barry Manilow's standup piano-playing style, which he labeled "shitheaded."

Writing in *Rolling Stone*, Stephen Holden commented, "A bantam, hyperkinetic Rocky Balboa onstage, Joel works audiences into a lather of adulation with the snappy calculation of a borscht-belt ham. As cockily aggressive as Sammy Davis Jr., he lards his performances with schtick that usually includes impersonations of such genre greats as Elvis Presley, Bruce Springsteen, et al."

The mimicry Holden observed is one of the outstanding items in Joel's variegated bag of tricks. At the Mar y Sol Rock Festival in Puerto Rico in 1972, Billy made a strong impact with his dazzling impersonation of Joe Cocker.

At the end of his performance, Joel

Tony Frank/Sygma

will often instruct his audience, "don't take any shit from anybody." He told Dave Marsh what he meant by this. "I've found audiences over the years have been used to accepting shit from performers; one token encore, then the announcement: 'They have left the building'. The jive performers give an audience—people pay $9.50 a ticket, the group goes onstage on automatic pilot.

"I've been on the road for eight years," he continued. "I've met a lot of rock stars. A lot of 'em have a lot of contempt for their audience. They really think they're a bunch of jerks. When I'm onstage, the main thing I'm thinking about is, I want them to feel like that $9.50 was worth eighteen dollars, nineteen dollars. Like they walk away up. Like I didn't give them, I didn't give them no shit. I happen to think that they're into me, they have a certain amount of intelligence. I don't know, maybe I'm idealistic. I like to think that people are smart."

Joel's sometimes sweaty energy and athletic magnetism have a visual impact that is an essential part of his appeal as a concert attraction, and they also work well on television. He became one of the growing number of recording artists who hawk their wares via TV ads in which they themselves appear.

A white-jacketed Billy, perspiring behind his piano on stage while singing "Just They Way You Are" was not only a spot for his platters but was picked up by many radio stations to illustrate visually what one could expect to hear at their frequency.

An extremely amusing and forceful ad featuring strains from "Movin' Out (Anthony's Song)" had a very pugnacious Billy, resolute after a tiff of some sort, slamming the door to his apartment and striding to a waiting car with the top down. He and a few mates then proceeded to "move out."

A recent spot for the *52nd Street* album is the first in which Billy plays directly to the camera. Writhing and grimacing in what appears to be a recording studio, Billy spits out the acerbic lyrics to "Big Shot," one of the singles from the album. Like the musical delivery, his physical performance is intensely dramatic; it is one of the more gripping record pitches on television, and it is less than a minute long.

Even before fans had gotten through consuming *The Stranger*, Billy Joel was ready with its successor.

The cover of *52nd Street* shows Billy in track shoes, jeans, and loosened tie, slumped against a building in the evening. He is brandishing a cornet; if he plays it at all, he has certainly refrained from doing so on record thus far. The photography correctly evokes a connection between Billy and the streets, underlining his image as urban gadabout, as an observer of the ever-changing scene.

By the 1978 release date of *52nd Street,* rock performers who drew their inspiration from a city environment were becoming more dominant voices in the music business. The pulse of the city was the lifeblood of a varied spectrum that included Bob Seger, Bruce Springsteen, Patti Smith, Meat Loaf, and the Ramones.

The attempt by the already popular Joel to incorporate this element into his broad-based appeal seems very clear. According to his official Columbia biography of the time, "Billy Joel is closer to the streets than ever, drawing from his environment sharp lessons of survival, empathy for the class struggle, and ironic glimpses at the frustrations and fulfillment of love."

"I still kick over garbage cans," observes Joel in the same document. "It's a way of life."

Perhaps choosing the title *52nd Street* is part of Joel's continued public love affair with New York. There is at least one additional possible meaning, intentional or otherwise; 52nd Street is the address of Columbia Records and CBS, Inc. Joel has indicated that at least part of the reason for the title *52nd Street* is that the entrance to A&R Studios is on that street. He gave much thought to naming the album *Stiletto,* after a song he likes a great deal, but he decided not to give the album "that kind of stigma."

For *52nd Street*, the cast of producer Ramone and musicians Stegmeyer, DeVitto, Cannata, and Khan is back. The entire cast (noted as "The Lords of 52nd Street" for this outing) includes a host of heralded guest stars, among them Donnie Dacus and Peter Cetera of Chicago to sing background, jazz great Freddie Hubbard on trumpet, guitarist Eric Gale of Stuff and hundreds of jazz-fusion sessions, master percussionist Ralph MacDonald, and guitarists David Spinozza and Hugh McCracken.

Billy, not the most loose-lipped of rock stars, did supply a few comments about a few of the *52nd Street* songs in his Columbia biography. "Until the Night" is "my tribute to the Righteous Brothers and the Phil Spector sound," for whom "Say Goodbye To Hollywood" was an earlier homage.

"Stiletto," says Billy, is "a really dark song, about masochism, emasculation." The author calls "Big Shot" a great hangover song" and suggests that "Honesty" is "not a really popular sentiment."

52nd Street is, of course, the first and only album Billy Joel recorded in his relatively new capacity as one of the half-dozen biggest stars in the music business. However, that reassuring status doesn't seem to have affected his approach at all. There is no evidence of complacency on *52nd Street*; there is no playing it safe. Joel confronts his material with the same freshness and fervor that got him his stardom in the first place. It is not uncommon for a superstar, right after he gets to that lofty pinnacle, to more or less tread water or run in place for another album or two—to regurgitate the same stuff that has proved popular in the past. Such a cop-out doesn't suit Billy Joel; he has got new things to say and new ways to say them. Still, he does have one advantage he didn't have previously; he can now be assured that people are ready and willing to hear whatever he *does* choose to spring on them.

"Big Shot," commencing with Steve Khan's sinister, slashing guitar and Liberty DeVitto's clashing cymbals, is Billy Joel at his nastiest. His voice oozes with contempt, with nary a trace of sympathy for this big shot.

"Big Shot" is a tale of contemporary decadence and urban nightlife. It's never clearly stated that this big shot is a woman, but we can assume as much. Her major sin, in the singer's eyes, is her having made a spectacle of herself by celebrating way beyond normal human limitations.

This big shot is quite a big shot; she's got a limo and the finest fashions (Halston) and knows the gang at Elaine's (where the talented and gorgeous hang out). And she engages in the trademark indulgences of the young, lovely, the wealthy, and the shallow:

*"Dom Perignon in your hand
And the spoon up your nose."*

She may have sparkled in the spotlight the night before, but she didn't know when to quit, and the next morning most of it is a foggy memory. Billy is unmoved; no matter how much her brain burns and her eyes are bloodshot, he swears:

David Gahr

David Gahr

Joseph Sia

*"Go on and cry in your coffee
But don't come bitchin' to me."*

"Big Shot" is a song of unbridled anger, and Khan's guitar, the featured instrument here, is an implement of meanness. Joel's disdain for the kind of life led by this big shot could not be more strongly expressed, unless he were to go a step too far and suggest she slash her wrists. He doesn't do that, but "Big Shot" is a powerful commentary about young folks who attain sudden money and notoriety. Joel is part of that class, but clearly he does not subscribe to all of its pasttimes.

Perhaps what he finds lacking in that context is honesty, which he searches for in the next song, aptly titled "Honesty." It seems to be the most elusive commodity imaginable.

With full orchestral backing, Joel the balladeer sings of how so many feelings—tenderness, sympathy, et al—are easy to come by, while total truthfulness seems impossible to find. As his search for it proceeds, Joel's voice graduates from soft plaintiveness to severe anguish. There is so much he can get, but he's looking for the ultimate from one special person: "All I want is someone to believe." The believing is, of course, double-edged. He wants someone to understand and accept what he is putting forward, but he also wants that someone to be a person whose actions, words, and feelings he can accept at face value. While that is a tall order, it shouldn't be impossible to fill. Alas, it appears to be.

From a musical standpoint, "Honesty" isn't remarkable; it is quite simple. But a fancier framework might have masked the emotional trauma Joel projects here. "Honesty" is a cogent treatise on a matter that is every bit as rare and crucial as Joel claims it is.

"My Life" is the third song on the first side. Of all Billy Joel's tunes, only

"Just The Way You Are" has received more airplay. "My Life" has come to be seen as Joel's personal anthem; in years to come it may mean the same thing to him as "My Way" does to Frank Sinatra or "I Gotta Be Me" does to Sammy Davis, Jr. The sentiments are very much the same. Joel sings "My Life" with pride and swagger and makes an adamant plea to be left to his own devices without having to endure the judgements of others.

The song opens jauntily with Stegmeyer's pulsating bass and a variety of electric and acoustic keyboards. The first verse tells of an old friend who has just contacted Billy; he's packed it in, left his business and home, and split for the West Coast because "he couldn't go on the American way." He couldn't adhere to codes of behavior other people set up for him. This old pal is presented as a prime example of why it's healthier to take your own independent path in this life. It is also a springboard for Billy's statement of his own individuality. "This is my life," he boasts, "go ahead with your own life and leave me alone."

People will tell you what you can and cannot do—often in a garble of inconsistency that makes more confusion than sense. As an example, Joel here notes that people will inform you where and with whom you can sleep. That's immaterial; what's ultimately important is the fact that "you wake up with your own self." And it is your own self whom you must answer to and live with. So you'd better be pleased with what your own self elects to do.

The most vital matter about a statement like "My Life" is that it be delivered with the strength and courage of conviction, and Joel does that and more. He tells us "this is my life" in a way that impresses us with his character as much as a proud peacock impresses us as he struts in full display of his feathers. Billy Joel has made his point.

The first three songs on *52nd Street* all had major statements to make. "Zanzibar," up next, is more along the lines of good fun. Musically and lyrically, "Zanzibar" is an adventurous trek into the exotic wild—although it is in fact a journey to a nightclub.

The hero of "Zanzibar" is a young man of seemingly limited means, but he apparently possesses all the assets he needs for a good evening of gallivanting. He immediately contrasts himself with Muhammad Ali, who "dances and the audience applauds." He hasn't got such an enormous following; he's "just another face at Zanzibar."

But this young crowd-pleaser is only trying to please a crowd of one, anyway. The object of his affections is a waitress who seems to be from the wrong side of the tracks but whose smile is very much *on* track. It is his fervent wish, and his bold prediction, that when the night is over she will be waiting at home and will "pull the curtains down for me."

The extremely contemporary Joel takes episodes out of current headlines—these from the sports pages—and compares his situation to that of baseball superstar Pete Rose and the feudin' New York Yankees. The baseball metaphor is heavy but apt; he is aiming "to get to second base / And I'd steal it if she only gave the sign." He's confident, and time is on his side: "She's gonna give the go ahead / The inning isn't over yet for me."

Joel is drawing us into this guy's amorous adventures, but he is simultaneously bringing us into the heady atmosphere of Zanzibar itself. While the protagonist sits back with his beer and ponders his rosy future, we're given a nifty taste of smoky nightclub jazz—first an easy piano and vibes passage by Joel and guest performer Mike Mainieri, then an archetypal hot-jazz riff by Stegmeyer (probably playing an acoustic standup bass) and trumpet legend Freddie Hubbard, whose solo is quick-fingered and nimble-lipped.

The young hero, given time to contemplate the mission that waits him, emerges more brash than ever. In his old man's car, he'll be heading out to that waitress's quarters in due time, and no doubt his romantic goal will be achieved.

"Zanzibar" is lively, picturesque, and atmospheric; Joel brings us deep into the scene he has drawn. We are there amid the bustle and beer, and we are sharing this kid's giddy expectations. "Zanzibar" is a slice of life that intrigues us and commands that we participate. We would do so willingly.

"Stiletto," which launches side two, is about a most deadly woman, a kind of Jackie the Ripper. Her cutting, described in gruesome detail by Billy, is purely metaphorical. No actual blood is shed, but her effect is probably just as devastating.

"Stiletto" opens with the lonely, urban street-sound of Cannata's tenor sax. The lonely city stillness is altered by a repeated three-note combination at the very lower end of Billy's piano that creates an impression of some stealthily creeping menace. The evil comes closer on a wave of finger snapping and finally emerges on the heels of Joel's discordant "Chopsticks" piano passage.

This is just the beginning of a brilliantly structured tune. There is no lead guitar here, but instead an oft-repeated harsh and jarring chord. And when Billy sings "she cuts you once, she cuts you twice," his piano punctuates each slash.

The knife-wielding metaphor continues throughout the entire song. Here's a woman who does serious, deep damage —more spiritual and emotional then physical—but is such a skillful manipulator that she always comes back and has little trouble reestablishing things *status quo ante bellum*. In fact, she can have you "pleadin'/With your insides bleedin'/'Cause you deep down want some more."

The lady gives this guy whatever he wants—however perverse that may be—but even while she's being her sweetest, she "searches for the vein." She's so skilled with her psychological stiletto that "You don't even see the blade."

Is the man in "Stiletto" being admonished for being so masochistic, so ineffectual, or are we to believe that the conniving female is so remarkable that she'd be worth the high emotional price for anyone? The former would seem to be true, but in either case there is no doubt that we are meant to admire this lady for her marvelous abilities, if not for her intentions.

Part way through the song, Joel and company do a musical about-face, and Billy supplies some free-form keyboard improvisation while Stegmeyer stays in stride by plucking furiously up and down the neck of his bass. The interlude is excellent connective tissue, for out of it emerges Cannata's saxophone. This time, however, it positively screams in anguish, obviously at the pain caused by the woman with the stiletto.

After a few more verses, "Stiletto" ends with a reprise of the beginning—Billy's staccato piano. We were warned of the lethal lady's arrival, and it seems we are being apprised that she is about to go on the warpath once again. We are on the lookout.

"Stiletto" is a thoroughly realized undertaking; music and lyric work hand in hand to make Joel's theme as vivid as possible. Always interested in relationships, he is a frequent commentator on their dark side. And "Stiletto" seems to suggest that the one who allows his partner to perform such acts of mental cruelty is as much to blame as the one who is cruel.

"Rosalinda's Eyes" is very light and

United Press International

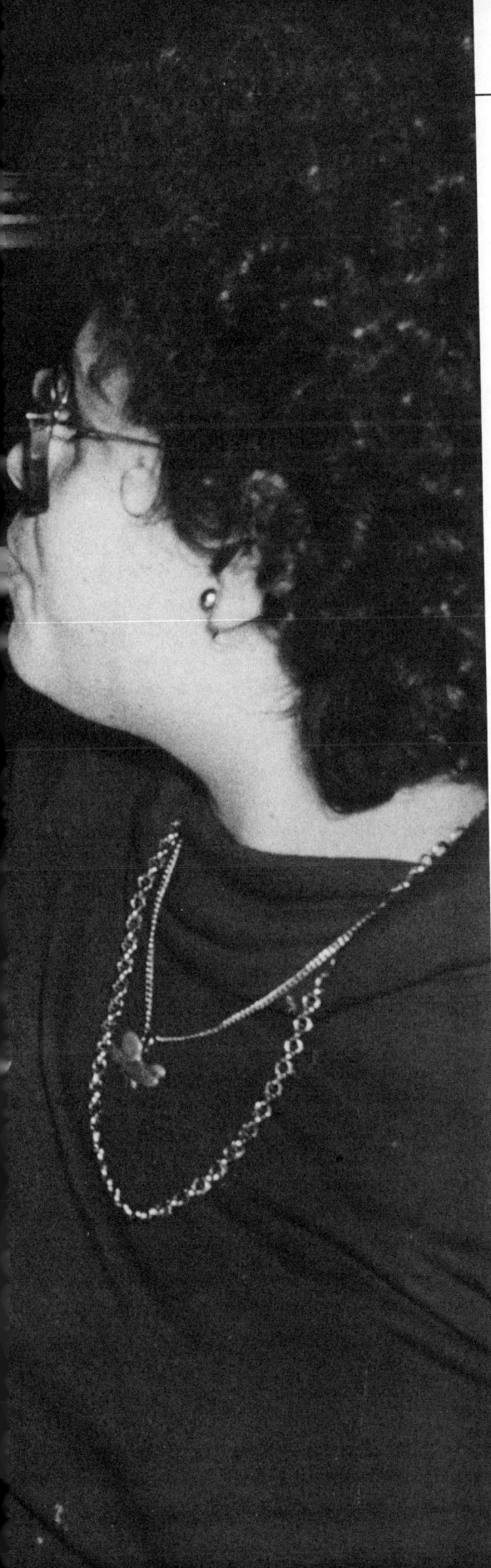

very Latin; the electric piano and organ that give the song its foundation are indeed mellow, however overused that word may be. Ralph MacDonald guests with some Caribbean percussion, and Hugh McCracken plays a nylon-string guitar—the kind that makes each note very distinct and precise. The festive flavor of "Rosalinda's Eyes" comes largely from the sweet, high-pitched sounds of George Marge's sopranino recorder.

The hero of "Rosalinda's Eyes" plays in a Puerto Rican band in Spanish New York; he yearns for an exotic life and stardom, but what he gets instead are "Union wages, wedding clothes," and relative obscurity. He'll never get to Havana, but he can get his glimpse of Cuba, which he can find in the lovely Rosalinda's eyes.

Simple, romantic, Latin, and very pretty, "Rosalinda's Eyes" is a ballad which fits in nicely here on side two of *52nd Street*. Its gentleness is 180 degrees removed from "Stiletto."

"Half A Mile Away" is a joyous celebration amid R&B trappings. Stegmeyer plays a punchy Motownish bass, and Dave Grusin has been enlisted to orchestrate a horn section that would do any of those sixties Sam and Dave-ish soul revues proud. The proceedings are very up tempo.

"Half A Mile Away" is a demanding vocal test for Joel, but he is up to the challenge. There are falsetto passages, phrases that approach scat singing, and about as many rhythm changes as you can count on both hands. Yet Joel never misses a beat or a note; and he sings it all as if he's having a ball. His confidence in singing ability is well earned; it's also a pleasure to listen to.

The subject of "Half A Mile Away" is a young soul who leads a kind of double life. To his family he's hard-work-

Billy with Phoebe Snow

ing and clean-living, a basic solid citizen. But he lives for the nights when he can sneak out and cavort with his more loose-living friends—like Geo, the little guy who joins him on the corner for a bottle of cheap wine.

This is a tale of simple, hedonistic pleasures, well earned by a working man. Those are the kinds of things a fellow can really revel in, just as Joel and his musical cohorts revel in performing "Half A Mile Away."

The epic of *52nd Street* is the 6:35 "Until The Night." For some tastes, this track alone is worth the price of the record. And when Billy Joel talks about his desires to become more sophisticated musically, there are those who would hope he means an album full of achievements like "Until The Night." It is a popular song on a mammoth scale, a sort of musical shot at the Great American Novel.

It works; it is a successful blend of so many elements that it almost qualifies as a history of twenty years of rock in less then seven minutes. Actually, perhaps the only component absent is electric lead guitar. But the sound of "Until The Night" is so full and rich that it isn't missed for a moment. "Until The Night" is the kind of song that really blossoms on headphones. If you've got them, use them; they may be the only device that can pick up every one of the countless activities going on in this number.

The first notes of "Until The Night" are a solid, low-end-of-the-scale piano foundation, but the first surprise is the vocal. It doesn't sound at all like any Billy Joel singing we've ever heard before. Your initial reaction might be to glance at the credits to see who the guest vocalist is. But the husky crooner is Billy, all right; we shouldn't forget what a capable mimic he is. There are several things about "Until The Night" that bring to mind the Righteous Brothers, the nonsiblings of "You've Lost That Lovin' Feeling" fame. In these opening moments, Billy sounds very much like Bill Medley, the darker, deeper-voiced member of the twosome—and later on, he will resemble none other than Bobby Hatfield, the blond tenor-partner of Medley.

Some writers, in discussing "Until The Night," have made comments about its similarity to the productions of Phil Spector. Spector's name frequently crops up in reviews when a recording artist forsakes the normal guitar-bass-keyboard-drums line-up for more lavish surroundings. It hasn't been stated for publication whether Joel and Phil Ramone were consciously emulating Spector. However, there is at least one more reason why Spector comes to mind here—he was the producer of the Righteous Brothers in their halcyon days.

In the complexity of "Until The Night," everything works. Robert Freedman's strings are florid but never overbearing, and his muted horns sound very much like the brass in old Gene Pitney tunes, notably "24 Hours From Tulsa." Hugh McCracken's nylon-string guitar lends the sound of what seems to be a half-dozen Spanish guitarists. And if there were any danger of things getting too exotic or ethereal, the necessary earthiness comes once again from Cannata. When the drama of "Until The Night" demands it, Richie is ready with his saxophone—at the exact moment that the impassioned pipes of singer Joel can use the added emphasis. Cannata is one of those rare individuals whose playing can literally send chills down your spine.

Something should also be said here about Liberty DeVitto's drumming. Never flashy or excessive, DeVitto is the cement that holds the proceedings together. His performance on "Until The Night" is typical of his appropriate re-

Charlyn Zlotnik

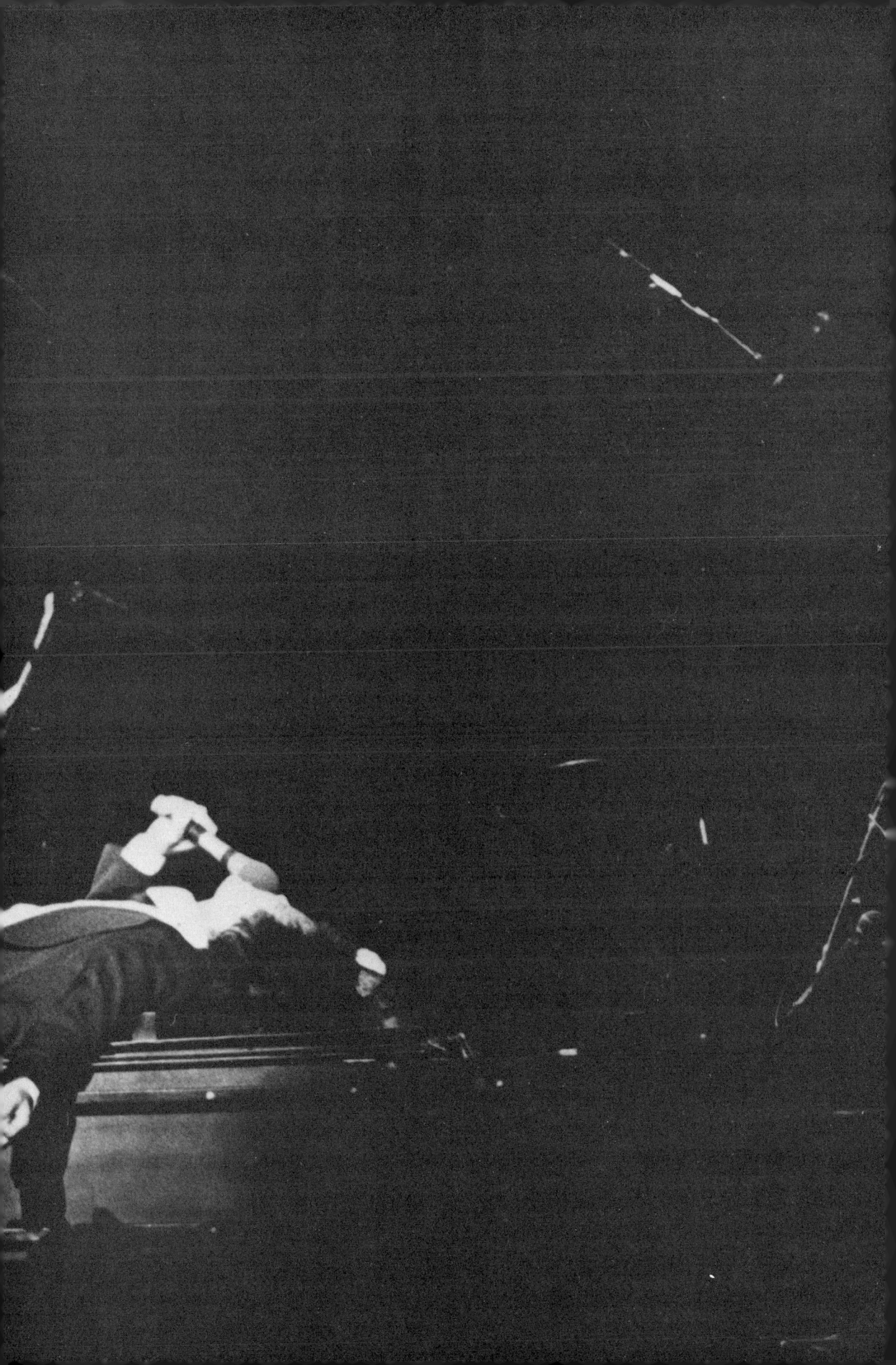

straint. He plays mostly on the rims and cymbals, but lightly; he is not a basher. He's a precision player who makes every note count; on this track almost every sound he makes is a comma, period, or exclamation point.

In his adopted baritone, Billy may be posing a bit, but the pose proves effective. It adds heroic stature to his character, a kind of stolid man of few words who says things like "Today I do what must be done." This is a Gary Cooper, or John Wayne.

The story of "Until The Night" is simple enough; the morning comes and a man and woman bid each other adieu before going off to perform their separate duties of the day. The day seems interminably long; the one desire, the chief consolation, is to get back into each other's arms when the sun goes down.

Time passes; age creeps up. Other loving couples come and go. With the time apart come uncertainties:

*"Today we'll be unsure,
is this what we believe in
And wonder how can we go on"*

could be a double-edged comment. They could have doubts about the value of what they do all day, but they may also be unsure about whether what comes at the end of the day means as much as it is supposed to.

That latter doubt disappears, however, when the day *does* end. The most gripping moments of "Until The Night" may come as the hero makes his way back home to his woman. If Billy Joel can project the same sense of drama and urgency with a movie script as he can with his own lyrics and notes here, he'll be an actor of the first magnitude.

The journey back through the night is recounted in step-by-step detail. His sensations change; the closer he gets to home, the more he comes to life ("I'm just beginning to feel"). When the sense of erotic splendor can no longer be expressed in mere human terms—that's when Cannata's sax comes in, enforcing the popularly held notion that the saxophone is the most sensuous of musical instruments.

A total triumph of composition, performance, and production, "Until The Night" is too complex to be a Top-40 single, but it became an FM favorite and, as time passes, it may become, along with "My Life," the reason why *52nd Street* is remembered. Putting together "Until The Night" was the single biggest musical task Billy Joel had tackled, and he didn't stumble. This may be his finest recorded song; it is certainly the one that best demonstrates the high level and variety of his musical abilities.

The silence after "Until The Night" lasts so long that one imagines the record is over. Finally, after the pause, we hear strains of the title song, "52nd Street," which is an afterthought and something of an anticlimax. It's a brief ditty about generating heat—mainly of the musical kind—on Fifty-second Street. By itself, the song isn't too memorable, but it could be seen as a kind of epilogue. After all, through eight previous tunes, Joel and his band did "generate a lot of heat . . . on 52nd Street."

The release date of the *52nd Street* album may have seemed premature; after all, *The Stranger* was still riding high on the charts. In retrospect, however, the timing is just one of the many components of a career that has been handled brilliantly, at least since 1977.

Joel had put together a long streak of chart-making singles from *The Stranger*; although the album was still selling, it was essential for purposes of continued Top-40 radio airplay to come forward with the new material. So whereas progressive album-oriented listeners might be wondering why Joel was in such a hurry, he was in fact doing just what he had to do to keep that singles winning-streak going without interruption.

Nevertheless, *52nd Street* does seem slightly rushed; it does not appear that quite as much time and effort and care went into it as were given to its predecessor. Joel did get his hits, including one song, "My Life," that has wedged itself firmly into the public consciousness. And Joel produced another track, "Until The Night," that qualifies as a genuine work of art in contemporary music.

On the whole, however, *52nd Street* is not quite equal to *The Stranger,* but that's not really a negative assessment. *The Stranger* is a masterpiece, a nearly perfect record. *52nd Street* is quite good and pleasant to listen to. And it gave Billy Joel fans just what they wanted— more Billy Joel songs. It is not, however, a great album.

52nd Street has kept the Billy Joel hit-singles streak very much alive; thus far, "Big Shot," "My Life," and "Honesty" have been staples of AM radio.

Susan Elliot, in *High Fidelity,* wrote that the material on *52nd Street* seemed "seasoned," thanks to Billy's "own sense of artistic confidence." To his own mind, he had come of age as a creative force, and with that feeling came "a new freedom of musical exploration." Coupled with producer Phil Ramone, Billy sought to diversify, and jazz became a bigger part of his sound.

Elliot also suggested that *52nd Street* contained ample evidence that as a pianist, Billy was tough to rival. She said "his ability to turn that instrument into a rhythm section's strongest anchor ("Zanzibar") and the next minute sound like a self-contained chamber orchestra ("Honesty") continues to be one of the most humbling aural experiences for all pianists—amateur and professional."

In *Stereo Review,* Peter Reilly suggested that Joel was influenced by the "blue-collar, lower-middle-class sociology" of Hubert Selby, author of *Last Exit To Brooklyn,* a gruesome and grisly tale of urban nightlife. However, Reilly felt that Joel, in the same "nightmarish city-scape," could find "a heartening amount of humanity, lots of hope," and "a kinetic high-spirited humor about people and the situations they find themselves in."

Stereo Review had given *Piano Man* a Record-of-the-Year award in 1974. In the same magazine, in January of 1979, Reilly said that Billy Joel's greatest strength is "his ability to show people as they are without lapsing into the condescending kitsch of 'All in The Family' or the spasmed frenzy of a Scorsese Grand Guignol."

Feature reviewer Don Shewey called the album cover "dumb for its 'Rocky' pose and added, "Joel has always been an easy target for his arrogance, pretentiousness, hyprocrisy, and on *52nd Street* he's still showing them off."

Joel's stuff, Shewey contended, is "calculatedly commercial music. It's pretty good music, mind you, in that its merits for the most part disguise its calculations, but it is still music that is meant to sell rather than to say something."

Shewey, however, was stunned by at least one of the *52nd Street* tracks. "On the whole, the friction from Joel's pretentious clashing with his accomplishments make for more excitement than the smooth surfaces of the likes of Stephen Bishop," he noted. "It also produces 'Until The Night', which cops unoriginally from Phil Spector, treads on Bruce Springsteen's night-as-salvation mythology, and steals Clarence Clemons's saxophone as mystical/erotic clarion —and *which* is the greatest fucking record Billy Joel has ever made. Like a

David Gahr

cross between the Righteous Brothers's 'You've Lost That Lovin' Feeling' and Springsteen's 'Incident on 57th Street', it is a majestic confrontation between heart-rending passion and inevitable tragedy, 6:39 of thrilling emotional turbulence."

The final verdict of Stephen Holden, writing in *Rolling Stone,* was that *52nd Street*, "though far from great, boasts much of the color and excitement of a really good New York street fair."

Holden suggests Joel is "the quintessential postrock entertainer: a vaudevillian piano man and mimic who, having come of age in the late sixties, has the grasp of knowledge and the technical know-how to be able to caricature both Bob Dylan and the Beatles as well as 'do' an updated Anthony Newley."

Holden says Joel understands that "rock & roll was always a part of show business" and that it has "always been a species of popular music and not a totally separate art form."

Holden called Joel "a great show-business personality in the tradition of Al Jolson," distinguished by "bluntness, brashness, a middle-to-lower-middle-class fringer urbanity, and plenty of heart. Joel's is a sidewalk voice from the chorus of *West Side Story,* vending chutzpah." To Holden, he is also "every scuffling city boy who ever made it big, crowing with ego but also giving back his all."

CHAPTER 9

In the Mainstream

David Gahr

Billy's insistence that he is a "musician" before all else seems justified by the evidence at hand. While he obviously is not ignorant of commercial considerations and has an uncanny ability to make hits, he has always performed *his* kind of music. Unlike a faltering act like, say, the Bee Gees, he has not foresaken his own forte to work within an idiom that happens to be currently popular.

He hasn't gone anywhere near disco, even if that might expand his already swelling audience. Rod Stewart, for example, did that with *Blondes Have More Fun* and stood atop the album charts in 1979 for six weeks. Billy Joel, on the other hand, makes his money playing Billy Joel music.

He also avoids the kind of glossy overproduction, often in the form of cloying violins, that can turn otherwise decent material into syrupy dreck. He remains melodic, or he rocks, and at the best of times he does both.

Joel's ability to transcend critical indifference was well illustrated by the results of the 1978 *Rolling Stone* Reader's Poll. That magazine's critics had even failed to mention Joel in their awards voting a few weeks before. But the magazine's readers, older and more sophisticated than those of other rock music publications, selected Billy Joel as fifth in the "Artist of the Year" category behind Bruce Springsteen, the Rolling Stones, Jackson Browne, and the Who, all of whom were much more extensively

covered in the issues of the previous twelve months.

The readers tabbed *The Stranger* as the fifth best album, following *Some Girls, Darkness on the Edge of Town, Running on Empty,* and *Who Are You.* Joel was also fifth in the "Best Songwriter" category, behind Springsteen, Browne, Warren Zevon, and the Mick Jagger-Keith Richards duo. Surprisingly, Billy Joel finished third in the voting for "Top Male Vocalist," behind Springsteen and Browne but ahead of Jagger and Bob Seger. While rock pundits were downplaying the significance of Joel's contributions to contemporary music, discriminating listeners knew for themselves what they liked.

The newly minted *52nd Street* did make *Time* magazine's 1978 "Pick of the Holiday Season" list of popular music albums, compiled by Jay Cocks, who touted efforts by Keith Jarrett, Devo, Van Morrison, Southside Johnny and the Asbury Jukes, The Clash, Wings, Johnny Cash, and Al Stewart along with Billy's latest. Of *52nd Street* Cocks wrote, "McCartney's competition. Homegrown and nurtured on big-city streets, Billy Joel sings spiky ballads and ornery anthems about bitches, grifters, and bozos on the make. Pop with a punch."

"The funny thing is that I've been supporting myself and getting standing ovations for four years now," he told Jerome. Of the critics who were just now taking notice of him, positive and negative, Billy observed "now they're saying I've made it. I thought I made it a long time ago."

"There's a certain kind of elitism," Joel told Marsh in discussing his detractors. "Like if you're from the city and you just do urban music, it's cool. If you're from the country, the mountains of Tennessee, you're authentic. But if you're from the mainstream, you're vanilla, you're nuthin'. Which is bullshit because... a lotta people are."

If Billy's failure to fit into any recognized pop or rock category is any reason why many critics have not embraced him fondly, he's not upset about it. "I don't need that," he told Jay Cocks. "Long, learned reviews are just hard to read."

Billy's failure to take full advantage of regular public relations channels often irks the folks around him. "It kind of throws the record company off," he conceded to Susan Elliot, "because they think everybody is dying to be a rock star, and when somebody doesn't care much they think, 'Well, he won't play the game.'"

It is from other people that Joel the songwriter draws his inspiration. "I gotta draw from life, not from my own life, other peoples' lives. A lot of people think everything I write is autobiographic—that's not true. I'd be dead if everything I wrote was autobiographic, I'd have to be 80 years old. I take a lot from other people, I just use pronouns that might throw people off.... Everything is autobiographic in the sense that I've kind of vicariously imagined it or lived it—if I'm going to write about it, I have to have some kind of feeling for it, so it may be secondhand experience, but it's not necessarily *not* about me."

Billy's compositions and his piano playing may seem to be drawn from a variety of sources, and so they are. In addition to the years of classical lessons, he was obviously affected by the Long Island rock scene of the sixties, and very much by the Beatles. As Jay Cocks observed, "he counts for major inspiration the metric acrobatics of Dave Bruback's 'Take Five' and the seamless jazz fantasies of Oscar Peterson. He dreams of the day Ray Charles will pull one of the best songs out of the Joel portfolio, 'and I'll hear 'New York State of Mind' at the World Series.'"

In *Changes*, in the early 1970s, one-time rock critic Joel wrote kindly of Stevie Winwood and Keith Emerson, and he has spoken of Jimi Hendrix as a genius. "To me there's only a few of 'em," he told Marsh. "Jimi Hendrix was a genius like Mozart was a genius, George Gershwin, Aaron Copland, Bach."

The succession of Billy Joel hits was masterfully planned; while one was riding high, still fresh in the public consciousness, another song was released by the crafty folks at Columbia.

Billy Joel music was everywhere one turned. The general public hardly complained; they enthusiastically gobbled anything the record company put out.

A few souls did object to what they considered overkill. On one progressive FM radio station in New York, a deejay responded to a flood of requests for "My Life" by playing four Joel songs at the same time—and subsequently smashing a copy of "My Life" on the air.

If the walls of the Joel home were a bit bare, there were plenty of honors coming Billy's way that would look nice over anybody's mantle.

The Recording Industry Association of America, which certifies success in very tangible terms, gives platinum disks to an artist who sells more than one million copies of an album. In 1978, Billy Joel received two chunks of platinum, one for *The Stranger*, on January 18, and another for *52nd Street*, on October 23. He also received a gold single, for sales over one million, for "Just The Way You Are," on March 6.

Joel's solid accomplishments for '78 were clearly reflected in year-end album and singles charts. Only one performer had two LPs among the Top-Thirty for the twelve-month period, according to *Variety*, and that was Billy Joel. *The Stranger* was number two; only the blockbuster *Saturday Night Fever* soundtrack sold more. What might Mr. Joel

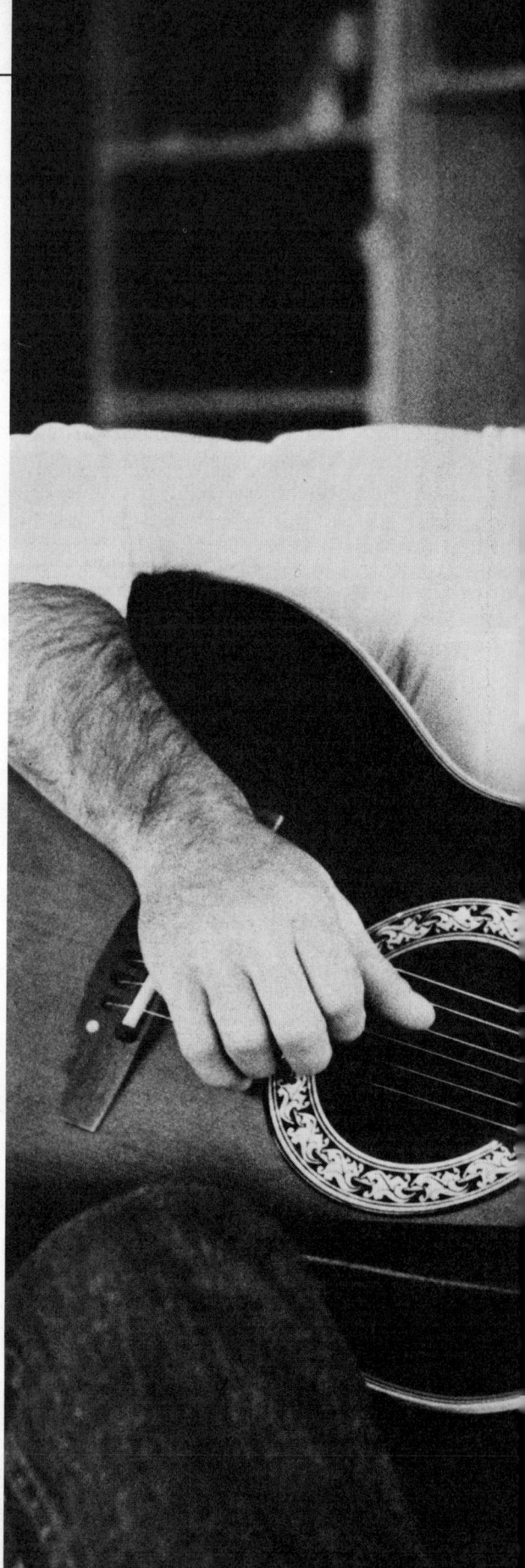

David Gahr

have done with the benefit of a movie tie-in like the Bee Gees had?

The Stranger even topped *Some Girls*, the ballyhooed Rolling Stones effort that received far more media attention. And, says *Variety*, the seventh best-selling album for 1978 was *52nd Street*, a record that had not even achieved its sales peak yet. *52nd Street* will undoubtedly appear prominently on 1979 year-end lists.

"Just The Way You Are" ranked 19th on 1978 singles lists, a sterling showing in the face of domination by the Bee Gees and their productions and compositions for other artists.

"My Life," not yet having achieved its highest chart positions, nevertheless placed 50th for the year.

The recording establishment itself, somewhat selective in its willingness to recognize achievement, did pay homage to Billy Joel with its Twenty-first Annual Grammy Awards. Two of the most important awards in the music business went to Joel for "Just The Way You Are," which *New York Times* critic John Rockwell later branded an "overtly, soppily sentimental ballad." Whatever it may be, Billy's peers voted it the "song of the year" and the "recording of the year," although they mysteriously reserved "male vocalist of the year" honors for Barry Manilow.

To readers of *Playboy*, a bit older and more mainstream in taste than those of most music publications, Billy Joel was as close to perfect as mortal man can come. From nowhere, he emerged to take first in three major categories in the poll.

Joel was chosen best male vocalist, with Jackson Browne taking second. He was also voted best keyboard player, beating the celebrated Keith Emerson, and he was picked as best songwriter, topping Bruce Springsteen.

For its fifth anniversary issue dated March 5, 1979, *People* magazine conducted a telephone poll of its readers (two-thirds of whom are under thirty-five) on a wide array of subjects. To the question "who is your favorite male singer?" the answer was Billy Joel, with Neil Diamond (a recent cover subject) placing second. As the editors noted, it was a matter of "Liking Billy Joel just the way he is."

Tony Frank/Sygma

CHAPTER 10

On the Road

In contrast with earlier statements, Joel now contends that "the essence of what we do is the road," which he gives greater importance than recording. He told Marsh, "the reason I'm doing what I'm doing is not to become a recording star—it's to go out on the road and play music."

By the beginning of 1979, Billy Joel was not yet a truly international pop star. He quickly set out to change that. In the winter, he embarked on a tour of Britain, France, and Scandanavia. On February 15, a packed house at Pleyel in Paris kept Joel on stage for a half-hour of encores after his blistering ninety-minute show. With a loosened thin necktie, leather jacket, jeans, and athletic shoes, Joel was acrobatic, peripatetic, and in fine voice. He gave the Parisians plenty to shout about.

And it wasn't just the capitalist world that was hearing the music of Billy Joel. In March of 1979, Joel along with Kris Kristofferson, Rita Coolidge, Stephen Stills, Weather Report, the Cuban group Irakere, and other Columbia artists, participated in the first U.S.-Cuba concert on Cuban shores in twenty years. It was a three-day affair at Havana's Karl Marx Stadium. As far as anyone knows, Billy did not dedicate "Big Shot" to Fidel Castro.

Joel's appearance on the final evening of "Havana-Jam-79" was, according to *New York Times* critic John Rockwell, "a stirring performance that brought the cheering crowd to its feet. Joel, the hottest American ticket in the three-day event, "drew the most fervent response of the entire festival."

Michael Putland/Retna

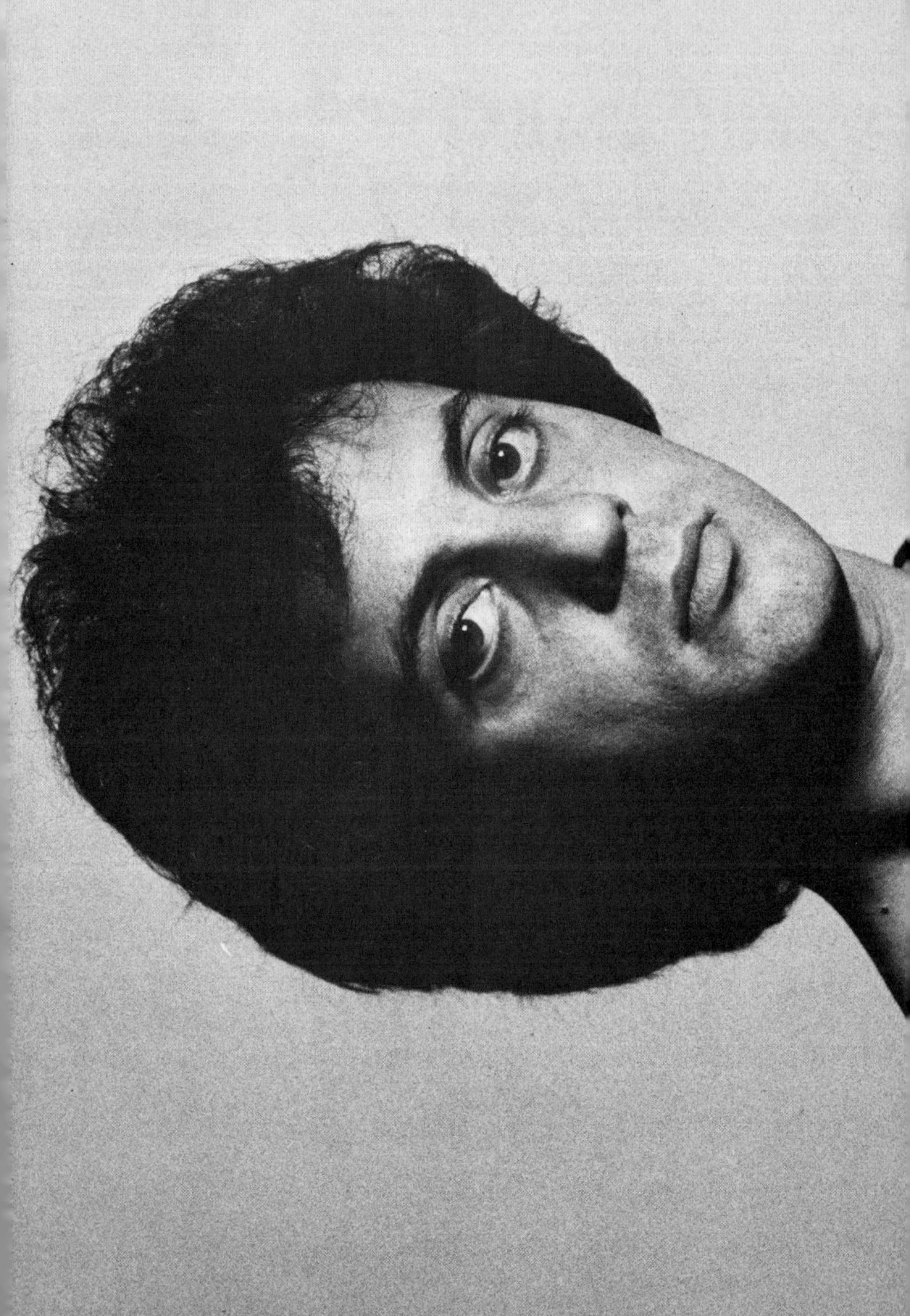

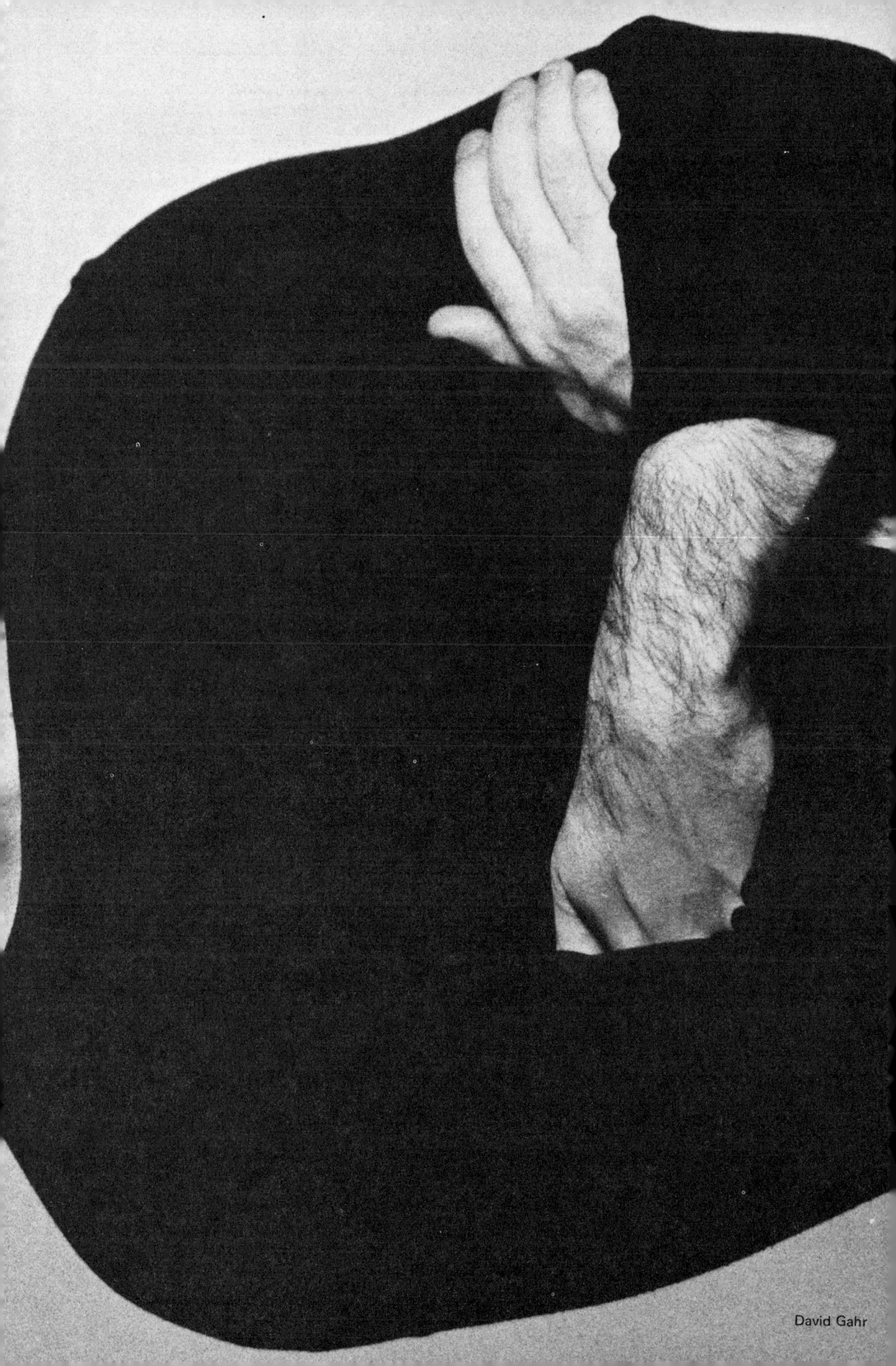

David Gahr

There had been some fears that Cubans might not know the Joel musical catalogue, but some actually spotted Joel T-shirts and, wrote Rockwell, "they screamed when his hits appeared, they danced in their seats, and they even tried to storm the stage at the end. It was just like home."

Rockwell believes that Joel and his band "seemed to play and sing with a special passion" and proved "that in the right context rock-and-roll still has the power to be subversive."

However, the *Times* writer also suggests that Joel's impact at the Havana fest may have been at least partly due to the brevity of his set, which lasted an hour. "His normal, two-and-one-half-hour set seems to drag on too long; his music simply isn't that interesting. In one hour, there's just enough of it for this case—15 minutes too much, even?—and the set is pared down to his very best songs."

Most of the concert was recorded for a possible film and album; Joel's portion was not. Of the decision for him not to be taped or filmed, Billy said, "I'm not down here on some capitalist venture. I'm here to play music for these people."

According to *People* writer Jim Jerome, Joel spent his spare hours reading Harrison Salisbury's mammoth book on Russia, *Black Night, White Snow,* and listening to Paul McCartney on cassette at the beach.

The visiting American stars did not exactly have complete run of the country. According to Joel, he and some friends were barred from entering an old Ernest Hemingway hangout "because they said we looked like hippies."

Some of the Cubans were familiar with Joel's music; they had heard it on Miami radio stations, and even an outlet as far away as Little Rock. For the young Havanans, Joel's appearance was historic. One fan told Jim Jerome, "We listen to him on the radio and when the weather is clear we can see 'Soul Train' on television. But now here's Billy. This is the most important thing to happen in twenty years."

For his appearance in Havana, Billy made the cover of *People*. The magazine's headline proclaimed, "Billy Joel rocks Cuba. He wasn't hijacked; Fidel invited him and Kris & Rita for a Havana Woodstock."

The festival wasn't a complete thrill for all the American participants. Communications were shoddy, conditions in living quarters were not of the luxury variety, red tape (in the form of paperwork) seemed endless, airport delays were extremely long, and some of the musicians even had to load their own baggage onto their departing jet.

There was scarcely time for sightseeing; there was, however, plenty of opportunity to hear Cuban music: That prospect was less than exciting for some of the Americanos. At one point, according to *The New York Times*, Liberty DeVitto fell to the floor of a bus and warned in anguished tones that if he heard one more conga drum he would run amok.

"I don't analyze it, I don't intellectualize it—I just do it," Joel said of his songwriting approach in an *Us* magazine piece. "I don't sit down and write troubadour-balladeer stuff. I go with the moment."

The *Us* article was part of a series heralding a return to romantic music. The cover featured Joel along with such luminaries as Barry Manilow, Andy Gibb, and Olivia Newton-John. Just how a substantial talent like Joel would feel in the company of such simpering lightweights is known only to himself. *Us* claimed, "there's an edge of urban toughness to Billy Joel's songs, but that only enhances the sometimes idealistic romanticism of his lyrics."

In *Rolling Stone*, Joel contended that he is not image-conscious when he's writing. "I'm just goin'. I work myself up into a state. For weeks I'm empty. I got nothin', I'm dry, I walk around, I'm the worst person in the world, I got stubble, I smoke, I drink, I get bombed, I curse at everything, I throw things, I think it's all over. And then I click. I don't analyze it, I don't intellectualize it, I just do it."

What of the nastier side of his lyrics? Billy noted to Timothy White "I've heard people say, 'My, he's full of vicious attacks'. But it's just meant to be the other side of a question. I'll write a love song, but then distrust the sentimentality and want to write about the bitter, sarcastic side. I don't want to write a totally mushy love song because there's always that 20% of love that's like a stab in the gut."

That Billy was one of the hottest tickets was made clear in a U.S. tour that followed his Havana appearance. The tour did not include a stop in New York City. However, a Bronxville, New York, organization was offering tickets to a Joel concert in Providence, Rhode Island, and chartered bus transportation—for $35 per person.

"I've been trying to say *for years*, I've been successful for a long time," he told Marsh, "because I have been able to support myself as a musician since about the time I was twenty. Which is a miracle in itself. There're very few musicians who can support themselves just being musicians. So that's success. If you can support yourself being a musician, it's a miracle."

"The only difference that success means financially is that I can pay these people who have been working for me a long time, who weren't able to get peanuts in the old days and are now getting a financial return," Joel has commented.

"I don't give a damn, but it's good for the guys in the band who can now make some money. Or we could put it into production and have a better show, put more into sound, put more into lights, get better equipment. That's all I'm interested in—it does make a difference."

To hear him tell it, Joel has learned to control his emotional ebb and flow pretty well. "I'm one of the most self-centered, happiest people." he confided to Marsh, "and it has nothing to do with money or success or anything like that. I know I'm okay. I been at the bottom, I know what it's like. I'm still gonna go for the top, but if I don't hit the top, it doesn't mean I'm at the bottom, it just means I'm not at the top."

"You just go with the moment," Joel has said. "I'll probably do music, as far as I can see, because I'm a musician. I'll always be a musician. Since I was four years old I've been a musician. So I don't want to stop doing that. I like it too much."

He explained to Maureen Early, "I want to be a musician all my life. The No. 1 thing doesn't really matter to me. The amount of money, the amount of record sales was never a motivation. There are a lot more songs I want to write. I want to get musically more sophisticated. I want to branch out into movie scores, Broadway plays, I want to do some acting."

By 1979, Billy Joel was dividing his home life between a comfortable Long Island estate and a newly purchased Manhattan apartment on East Fifty-seventh street, with a panoramic view from more than forty floors above the street.

The Joels' current Long Island home is a fieldstone and cedar edifice on 4.7 acres, near Oyster Bay. In January, Billy told *Newsday* reporter Maureen Early "When I was a kid, I used to ride my bicycle around this area. I always wanted to live around here, but I thought you

David Gahr

had to be a Kennedy or an Onassis for that. That's why I'm still walking around in a daze." The home includes a private gym and a studio with a sound-mixing machine.

The view from the Oyster Bay home stretches all the way to the hills of Connecticut. That fact is of some importance to Joel the artist: "It's like not having your mind walled in."

Oyster Bay is a cherished and enviable haven. With the possible exception of some communities on the far eastern end, it is the loveliest town on Long Island. Billy Joel is probably the second biggest name in the annals of Oyster Bay. For many years, it was the home of Theodore Roosevelt; his estate of Sagamore Hill is one of the higest points in Oyster Bay.

Older than most Long Island towns, Oyster Bay does not have assembly-line housing. It consists of individual estates on large lots of acreage. Many homes are of Tudor-style architecture; quite a few date back to Teddy Roosevelt's time.

And, of course, there is the beautiful Oyster Bay harbor. Protected on three sides, it is a tranquil inlet of the Long Island Sound, a soft blue vista that is easily visible from the front windows of many Oyster Bay houses.

To hear him describe it, Billy Joel, after achieving a degree of wealth and fame that is rare even in the rock music business, is still Just Plain Bill. "I still have a better time going to the Blarney Stone (a chain of working-class restaurants and bars) and listening to the old men talk about their war experiences." What he's saying sounds very much like the scene depicted on the back cover of *The Stranger.*

"Everybody has something that they're going through, something that they have to say, and I'm a good listener," explains Joel, whose listening ability

David Gahr

would at least partially account for his vast storehouse of subject matter. "When I go out I don't talk a lot. . . . It might be a Long Island thing, maybe it's a New York thing, I don't know. But you gotta be able to laugh and make fun of things and have a joke about it. If you take yourself too seriously you're a drag and it gets boring."

Observes Billy, "I liked the Beatles because they laughed at themselves all the time, they could make a joke. I take my music seriously but not the ramifications of it—'Well, let's go to Studio 54, hey'—it's more fun to hang out and do crazy things."

"I don't go to fancy clubs like Studio 54," Joel told Timothy White. "I prefer the 'underbelly' bars where I can dress crappy and ease in without somebody yelling, 'There's Billy Joel!' I'm not looking for the seedy side, like Tom Waits. I'm after the norm."

The future growth of Billy Joel could be one of the most interesting show business stories of the early 1980s. He has been so prolific throughout his career that it's not inconceivable that he will continue to release an album of original songs every twelve months—each one containing three or four hit singles, each one zooming on to the charts "with a bullet" just as its predecessor's mammoth sales begin to dwindle.

The excursions Joel has made into jazz on his last two albums could continue and perhaps make him the pioneer of a brand new popular-music form. Nowadays, anything that has elements of rock and jazz is loosely titled "fusion music"; but as Billy Joel keeps mixing those and other elements, he may "fuse" something the likes of which we've never heard before.

And Billy's announced intentions of branching out into Broadway and film work should be rewarding. His vitality and creativity have often dominated a stage for over two hours; he is an athletic, charismatic, and theatrical performer whose talents are at least of cinemascope dimensions. John Lennon, Mick Jagger, and Robbie Robertson have proven that a music idol's appeal can be translated to the screen, and Billy Joel may have a greater *physical* range than any of the others.

Whatever else Joel chooses to do, he will continue to put out records that sell millions of copies. He has joined that select circle of artists whose albums now are certified million-sellers even before the public has heard them.

As the seventies draw to a close and the eighties begin, Billy Joel is in perhaps the most enviable position of any American musician. All he ever wanted to do is make a living at music, and he won't *ever* have to worry about that again. He is a songwriter first, a man with an urge to put his thoughts and feelings down for the record. And the public, with its buying power, has said that it likes what Billy Joel has to say.

He has found his audience, and it is the biggest one enjoyed by any American recording star. For Billy Joel, superstardom is a relatively new phenomenon. But he is not a flash in the pan. He is a seasoned performer with solid skills who has had the time to mature personally and professionally. He can handle the successes, and the challenges, that the 1980s will bring.

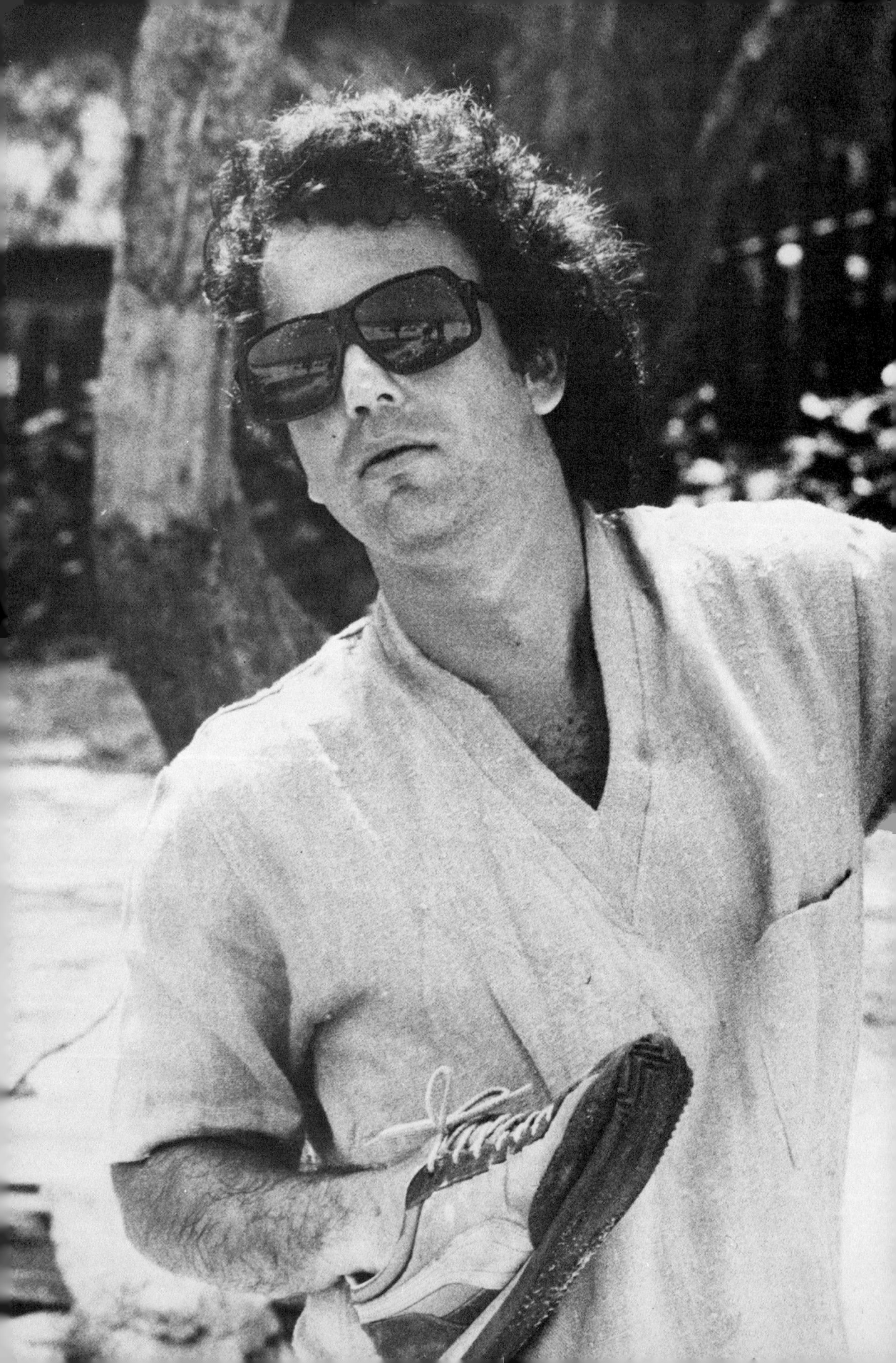

Discography

Cold Spring Harbor, Family Productions, FPS 2700 (1972)

    She's Got A Way
    You Can Make Me Free
    Everybody Loves You Now
    Why Judy Why
    Falling Of The Rain
    Turn Around
    You Look So Good To Me
    Tomorrow Is Today
    Got To Begin Again

Streetlife Serenade, Columbia, PC 33146 (1974)

    Streetlife Serenader
    Los Angelenos
    The Great Suburban Showdown
    Root Beer Rag
    Roberta
    The Entertainer
    Last Of The Big Time Spenders
    Weekend Song
    Souvenir
    The Mexican Connection

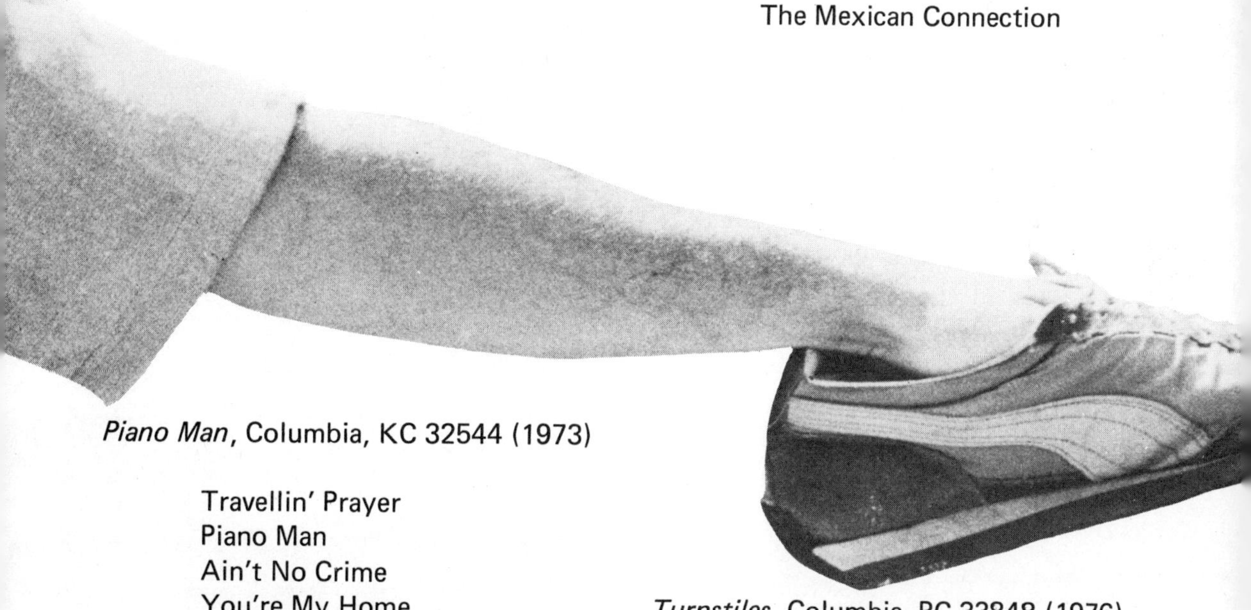

Piano Man, Columbia, KC 32544 (1973)

    Travellin' Prayer
    Piano Man
    Ain't No Crime
    You're My Home
    The Ballad Of Billy The Kid
    Worse Comes To Worse
    Stop In Nevada
    If I Only Had The Words
    (To Tell You)
    Somewhere Along The Line
    Captain Jack

Turnstiles, Columbia, PC 33848 (1976)

    Say Goodbye To Hollywood
    Summer, Highland Falls
    All You Wanna Do Is Dance
    New York State Of Mind
    James
    Prelude / Angry Young Man

I've Loved These Days
Miami 2017 (Seen The Lights Go Out On Broadway)

The Stranger, Columbia, JC 34987 (1977)

Movin' Out (Anthony's Song)
The Stranger
Just The Way You Are
Scenes From An Italian Restaurant
Vienna
Only The Good Die Young
She's Always A Woman
Get It Right The First Time
Everybody Has A Dream

52nd Street, Columbia, FC 35609 (1978)

Big Shot
Honesty
My Life
Zanzibar
Stiletto
Rosalinda's Eyes
Half A Mile Away
Until The Night
52nd Street

Chuck Pulin